Every
Good
Gift
sufficient
grace
in time
of need

With the compliments of
DR. JOHN W. LUCAS
President
"The Maranatha Evangelistic Association"
P.O. Box 1292, Calgary, Alberta   T2P 2L2
Phone: (403) 283-2263   Fax: 283-4061
E-mail: lucasjw@cadvision.com

This book is an abridged edition --
2 chapters are deleted
due to the publisher's
production difficulties

Every Good Gift

sufficient grace in time of need

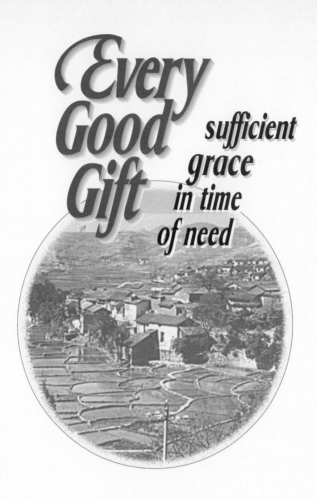

LINDA BAKER KAAHANUI

CHRISTIAN • LITERATURE • CRUSADE
Fort Washington, Pennsylvania 19034

CHRISTIAN LITERATURE CRUSADE
U.S.A.
P.O. Box 1449, Fort Washington, PA 19034

GREAT BRITAIN
51 The Dean, Alresford, Hants. SO24 9BJ

AUSTRALIA
P.O. Box 419M, Manunda, QLD 4879

NEW ZEALAND
10 MacArthur Street, Feilding

ISBN 0-87508-635-7

Cover design by
Evans Graphic Design
Camarillo, CA

Text set in Gilde
Titles set in Alexander

This printing 2000

Printed in the United States of America

CONTENTS

INTRODUCTION

BEFORE you jump into this book, I think two areas of explanation are in order. Many readers are already quite familiar with the events in China over the last 40 years. To you I apologize for the unnecessary verbiage. For others, I see the need to provide enough historical background to put the following stories into meaningful context.

In addition, many of you will be curious about the author's background and the origins of this book, so I humbly present some personal history.

Where does a story begin? You follow a plant to its roots—but if you pull at the root, you find that it goes deeper still. I suppose this book would not exist had not my paternal grandparents, Harold and Josephine Baker, boarded a steamer for China in 1911. I cannot say they had a particular love for the Chinese yet. But they loved God and shared Christ's desire to turn men from death to life. After a year-plus of language study in Anhui Province they set out, full of zeal to reach the most isolated pockets of humanity. They spent six months traveling up the Yangtze River, then climbed for two months through high mountains by yak caravan, finally arriving at the Tibetan border. They spent only five years there; but after burying two children, their hearts were firmly planted in China's soil. One child survived—my father, James.

The roots continue to run underground, but broad and deep. An American doctor in Batang said Grandma was dying and would probably not make it to Shanghai, much less America—so they headed home. In Tokyo, a surgeon found she had such massive adhesions he dared not even try to remove them. He gave her two weeks to live, but Jesus touched her a few days later and she was completely healed.

After five years in Ohio, Grandpa and Grandma experienced an intense baptism in the Holy Spirit and soon after felt compelled to return to China. They spent the next 27 years in the mountainous southwest province of Yunnan. "Adullam" was the name they gave to the home where, for many years, they took in hungry, diseased, and abandoned children who were found begging in the streets. These years were marked by a tremendous outpouring of the Holy Spirit upon the children of Adullam. My father grew up with these children until he left for college in the States at the age of 20.

By 1946, my father had married my mother, Marjorie Kennington—another China-born missionary kid—and they were headed back for Kunming, the capital of Yunnan province. My father's childhood friends were now pastors and teachers, co-laborers in the Lord. This turned out to be a short-lived but crucial time of sowing and watering what God would later bring to fruition.

In October of 1949, Chiang Kai-shek's Nationalist forces withdrew before the oncoming Communist army, throwing Kunming into panic. My parents and their two-year-old son were evacuated from Kunming to Hong Kong (five days before their second child was born). Six weeks later, the People's Liberation Army swept through the city. It would be 30 years before my parents heard from any of their dear Chinese friends and co-workers again.

Grandpa refused to leave and headed deeper into the mountains to work among the Kado tribal people. But in 1951, concerned that their presence would endanger the Chinese Christians, he and his wife left—to begin a new work among the Hakka people of Taiwan.

What happened during the next 30 years of silence? Here the stories in this book begin to put out shoots and grow.

At the end of 1949, Mao Zedong stood in Tiananmen Square

and announced that China was now a Communist country. He officially declared the people "liberated." For many of China's 800 million people, it was welcome news.

For decades, more developed nations such as Great Britain, the United States, Japan, Russia and others, had used military threats to impose a series of unjust and humiliating treaties on China. By expelling the foreigners—and all things foreign—the Communists promised to give the Chinese back their dignity, their "face."

Chairman Mao became a national hero. He offered hope for a better life to a country mired in poverty and famine. He assured the Chinese they would lift their heads in pride once again. Mao Zedong possessed an almost supernatural ability to command fanatical allegiance from the masses. Millions of Chinese zealously vowed their loyalty, their very lives, to this man. With an apparent mandate from the people, Mao began his great social experiment and the "bamboo curtain" came down.

Communism gave China a unifying purpose and a dream for the future. Later, especially during the Cultural Revolution, that zeal would be carried to excessive and tragic lengths. But perhaps we can understand what happened later by understanding the human spirit. Like breath itself, we all must cling to hope or die. The Christian always has his sure hope in Christ. Without this, the world has many sad examples of what man will do in the desperateness of his condition.

At first, the new regime paid little attention to the Church. When the Communist Party took control of China, there were fewer than one million Christians* in a population of 475 million —less than one quarter of one percent. The Party firmly believed that once it eliminated the presence and sustaining support of Western missionaries, Christianity would die its own natural death. By 1958, however, Party officials realized this belief system was not going away and that it posed a clear threat to the basic assumptions of Communist thought. The first major crackdown and wave of arrests swept through the Church that year. Almost over-

---

* Jonathan Chao and Rosanna Chong, A History of Christianity in Socialist China, 1949–1997, p. 34; CMI Publishing Co. Ltd., 1997, Taipei, Taiwan.

night, soldiers arrested thousands of pastors and teachers and shut down the churches. Christian schools were raided and closed. Anyone who had worked with a missionary was arrested on charges of "spying for a foreign government." Most were shot as "traitors." As persecution increased, anyone who could be connected with Christianity in any way became guilty of "anti-revolutionary" crimes. Thousands of Christians spent the next 20 to 25 years away from their families in prisons, labor camps and penal farms. Conditions were such that most were never heard from again. In 1980, over-crowded conditions led to the release of many prisoners who, due to age, were no longer considered a threat. However, they continued to live under house arrest with strict observation of their activities.

All of which brings me to Hong Kong, 1980.

My parents are working as writers and translators for an organization that publishes Christian literature and produces radio programming for China. The phone rings and the voice of a recent refugee from China asks, "Is there someone named 'Baker' there?" He says he has been going through the Hong Kong phone book, calling all churches and ministries. My parents race to a designated restaurant and sit down. They are joined by a couple they have never seen before. The woman pulls a photograph from her bag and holds it out. "Do you know these people?" Immediately, my parents recognize their former co-workers from Kunming. It is a time of tears and joy. The couple smiles. Mission completed! They have brought a message from Kunming. The man in the picture has told the couple, "When you find Pastor Baker, tell him we are alive. I know he will come." The man has spent 23 years in prison camp and is now free. There is a phone number to use in Kunming.

By this time, President Nixon had made his unprecedented trip to China and the "bamboo curtain" was showing a crack. Through a series of divine and mysterious interventions, the Chinese authorities granted my parents one of the first visas allowing a foreigner to travel unescorted in China.

As my parents visited many times over the next few years,

reunions with old friends were arranged by word of mouth. These friends told such incredible, beautiful stories of God's faithfulness to them in times of trial! Strikingly absent was any trace of bitterness, envy or regret. One thing came through—their passionate love for God.

But why write a book?—so many good books have already been written about the great revival in China. Since 1949, in spite of 40 years of systematic elimination and persecution, each Christian has multiplied into 100 Christians!* Every seminary in America likely has a small library, by now, documenting this phenomenon. All I know is that I felt strongly compelled by the Holy Spirit to write the stories down. So off I went to China with my mother.

---

* Estimates of the current number of Christians in China vary greatly and are highly controversial. Some researchers count only officially registered Christians. Others do not consider the registered Christians to be the true Church and so count only the underground, house-church believers. It is impossible, of course, to know the number of unregistered believers—and the figures tend to be deliberately understated so as not to alarm the government into greater persecution.

The Three Self Patriotic Movement (TSPM) is the government bureaucracy in charge of controlling Protestant religious activity in China on behalf of the Communist Party. According to the TSPM, there were approximately 700,000 Chinese Christians in 1949. In *The Resurrection of the Chinese Church*,† by Tony Lambert, the author quotes Donald Treadgold of the University of Washington as stating in 1973 that "the evangelicals' few Chinese converts were swallowed up by history, leaving . . . scarcely a visible trace." How wrong he was! Today, the Chinese government concedes the existence of 100 million believers, although outsiders estimate up to twice that number.‡

† Tony Lambert, *The Resurrection of the Chinese Church*, p. 9; OMF Books, Harold Shaw Publishers, 1994, Wheaton, Illinois.

‡ Jaime A. Florcruz and Joshua Cooper Ramo, "Inside China's Search for Its Soul," *Time* magazine, Vol. 154, No. 14, Oct. 4, 1999, p. 73.

Months of planning paved the way. Meeting places were set up, contacts arranged. For two months in 1988, we crisscrossed China. Christians came to tell us their stories, often secretly, often at great personal risk to themselves. I say this book has "old roots" because many of these people would never have spoken to a foreigner had it not been for the family's pre-war relationships; the Chinese place a great value on old and trusted friendships.

In 1991 and 1993, we gathered more stories and spoke to more witnesses to verify what we had already heard. It would take another long story to tell how God protected tapes and notes at every checkpoint. Every story in this book was related personally by the main character or by a minor character eyewitness. There are still so many more stories to tell!

I went to China armed with my list of questions: How does a Christian face tremendous sorrow and find joy? How does a Christian lose everything, yet keep a heart that is soft and filled with gratitude? How does a Christian stand all alone, with no one to encourage him, and remain true? I certainly saw myself as a "soft" Christian who knew nothing of real persecution. Didn't I have much to learn from my brothers and sisters who had been through the fieriest flames? Of course. But over time, I realized there was something much more important and more fundamental than any of these questions.

As I listened to tapes, read transcripts, and shared stories with others, I realized something. God was answering a different question altogether: "What does it mean to love God?" These might seem like stories about enduring, about forgiving, about courage or about miracles. But at the heart, they are simply stories about loving God with no conditions: no minimum daily blessing required, no comfort-zone boundaries, no expectation of anything other than to suffer for the sake of the one loved. When God is loved just for himself, what does he give in return? *Himself.*

The book is titled *Every Good Gift* for a reason. James 1:17 tells us "Every good gift and every perfect gift is from above, and comes down from the Father of lights . . ." (NKJV). All you have to read are the chapter headings to know where the book is going. God gives generously and graciously to his children a variety of gifts sufficient to meet the variety of our needs. But let me pro-pose that, as good and perfect as these gifts are, the *real* gift in each story is God himself.

As you read this book, you may be one looking for strength, for peace, for hope, for joy. Christians in the West have a huge "inspirational" industry that seeks to address these needs. We have Christian media, music, books, seminars and conferences, enter-tainment artists and more—all seeking to minister to these felt needs. Come meet some people who have *none* of the accouter-ments of Christianity . . . but have found everything they need in *God alone.*

1 *Chapter* 壹

THE GIFT OF FORGIVENESS

"The Lord Jesus, on the night he was betrayed, took bread, and when he had given thanks, he broke it and said, 'This is my body, which is for you. . . .' Anyone who eats and drinks without recognising the body of the Lord eats and drinks judgment on himself." 1 Cor. 11:23–24, 29

"BUT it still hurts!" my five-year-old wails. She is outraged at being asked to forgive her two-year-old sister for beating her on the head with a maraca. How do I explain grace to a small child?

Jesus prayed, "Father, forgive them . . ." even as he suffered. True forgiveness does not wait for the hurt to stop. It bears the pain and releases the offender from his debt.

Sometimes it is difficult to forgive, possibly because I don't realize the size of my own debt or the magnitude of my own pardon. Am I not a "nice" person? I have a chronic bias that elevates me above the sinfulness of others; but what a great leveler the cross is! The fact is, I am a full accomplice in the death of Jesus. We all stand equally guilty of his blood.

The cross is a debt I can never repay, an account I can never settle. I am wonderfully released from its burden by grace. If I will not release others of their debt to *me*—even when hurting, even when "right"—I return to the hell of a graceless world where wrongs must be righted and accounts must be settled. And what judgment will I drink upon myself? The anger of being owed, the self-pity of being wronged—these form my chains. Forgiveness is a gift of freedom: freedom from the law, freedom from my own sin, and freedom from the sins of others.

CANCELED DEBT

WITH a flick of her stick broom, Bright Moon sent her cooking scraps scuttling across the dirt floor and out to the yard. A greedy duck waddled from the bushes and snatched up the unexpected feast. Then Bright Moon slowly ran the broom across the entry again and again, until the hardpacked clay lost all traces of dripped water or spattered oil. Satisfied, she washed her hands and smoothed her hair.

Where was the gift from the missionary lady, the small bottle of a white lotion that smelled like summer flowers? Finding it, she rubbed it behind her neck. By saving it only for special occasions, she had made it last ten years. Bright Moon smiled to herself. *Mother would be proud.* She tied the bottle back up into an embroidered square of cloth—a wedding present from her grandmother—and tucked the precious bundle into a hole under her bed. Kwan was coming home!

Her husband could not earn enough to feed six children in the country. Their farm now belonged to "the people." A team of Communist cadres managed the farm, issuing orders from a windowless storage shed, now converted into a Party office. Five families lived under their once-spacious roof, trying to coax feeble vegetables from the depleted soil. Kwan made trips to the city whenever the labor committee gave him permission. In Shenyang, he could make a few extra pennies fixing shoes for pedestrians on the busy streets.

What a celebration there would be tonight! She eyed the plump duck and chuckled. Little Swan, her youngest daughter, could retire from her post as protector of the duck. The four-year-old took her job assignment seriously. Hearing her tiny voice shrieking at potential thieves always made Bright Moon laugh. She hoped Little Swan was not too attached to the duck now.

"Little sister, I have two more eggs!" Bright Moon's elder sister, Jade, lowered her head through the entry door, taking off her pointed bamboo hat as she spoke. Like all fieldworkers, she wore a scarf over her mouth and nose. As she worked at the knot behind her head with one hand, she handed Bright Moon two brown eggs with the other. "From our old teacher. He still has one chicken the committee hasn't confiscated. He says to welcome Kwan for him."

Bright Moon gratefully accepted the gift. She would miss the daily egg from her duck, but at least this meal would be memorable. She hugged her sister until Jade protested, laughing.

"Stop! They're just eggs, not precious jewels."

Bright Moon let go to wipe tears from her eyes. "It's having eggs, it's Kwan coming home, it's you and your husband safely back from your preaching. Jade, we have so much to be thankful for!"

Jade grinned. "Yes, we do, little sister. God is gracious to us. By the way, I invited Old Teacher to join us for dinner."

"Good. I'm sure he wants to hear everything about your last trip. Tell us again how you saw God heal a cripple and a deaf-mute, will you? I love that story!"

The two sisters finished their work and began to wait. They fed simple rice and soup to the children and waited some more. Beautiful dishes of food sat untouched. The sun went down and they watched by the light of their one, rationed, 40-watt bulb. Gradually, their excited giggles stopped and they sat staring out the door at the empty road. Occasionally they swatted at flies that hovered over the table. Finally, the children huddled together on the raised sleeping platform and fell asleep.

Bright Moon didn't dare speak. Her throat was so tight—if she opened her mouth at all, she knew she would cry. Where was Kwan? Her brother-in-law? Their dear teacher? She did not want to think about the possibilities. Pushing her fears from her mind, she shoved the dishes into a tight cluster and placed a ribbed mosquito tent over them.

"Well, it won't be hot, but it'll still taste good."

Jade's eyes widened. "Are you still thinking about food?"

Bright Moon bit her lip. She would not think about anything else! Only what a wonderful time they were going to have as soon as their loved ones arrived.

It started in the distance, just the faintest roar that rumbled softly through the village night. But as soon as the two women heard it, their breathing stopped and their ears strained. Jade dropped to her knees and soon Bright Moon knelt beside her. They held each other with clenched hands and began to pray.

Without seeing the mob, or hearing the words being shouted in the street, they knew. They realized they might never see their husbands again.

Life on Number Three Farm of Dongfeng County kept Bright Moon too tired to think much about the passing years. But that night in 1959, the night she last saw Kwan, returned often in her dreams.

The mob surging against the house, screaming children, the roof on fire. There is Kwan's face! Blood drips from his nose and eyes. A signboard hangs from his neck: "Enemy of the people." She tries to run to him. She tries to gather her children. They are dragging him away now. She must get to him! But they are beating her children. Little Swan's clothes are torn from her body and someone pulls a clump of hair from her head. Little Swan screams, "Mama! Mama!" Kwan is disappearing in the darkness.

"Stop!" Bright Moon woke from the dream, startled by her own voice. She rolled over, almost falling off her narrow bed of loose boards.

Her whole body still ached from yesterday's labor. Every day they dredged the riverbed, carrying mud in flat baskets suspended from a bamboo pole that crushed her knotted shoulders. They moved mud to fill one swampy inlet. Then, after months of struggling to meet some inexplicable deadline, they would get new orders. Dredge the new landfill and carry the mud back to the first location. It made no sense. Why did they call this a "farm" anyway? Nothing made sense.

But her children were alive and still lived with her. She thanked God daily for that. She prayed to see Kwan again. Would he recognize her? she wondered. Five years of hard labor and scant nutrition had changed her hair, her skin, the shape of her body. She rarely stood up straight; it hurt too much.

She massaged the gnarled clump of calluses on each strong hand. Where was that lotion now? The memory surprised her. She hadn't thought of that bottle in years! *Did it survive the fire? The looting?* She smiled at the irony of such a luxury. It was indeed another lifetime!

The afternoon sun reflected off the river in blinding slashes of light. Bright Moon squinted and spat out the grime that collected in her mouth. Mosquitoes swarmed to her perspiring skin.

"Bright Moon! Bright Moon!" Breathless, her unit comrade slogged toward her through knee-deep mud. "There is a transfer list. Posted on the truck. You're on it!" Gasping, she stopped. "Number Two Farm. You're going!" Delighted at her friend's good fortune, she watched for Bright Moon's response.

Bright Moon's heart pounded. She laughed, then cried. Kwan was at Number Two Farm! God had answered her prayer. They would finally be together.

"Go! Get your things. The truck leaves immediately. They already have your children in the grain yard."

"Yes, yes. I'm going." She felt delirious.

Bright Moon's tears washed little trails down her muddy face. Her friend laughed. "Clean up first, or Kwan won't be so excited."

By day, Bright Moon shoveled manure and herded cattle. She rarely saw Kwan. His unit raised bees. But they petitioned for living quarters as a family. Finally, the farm committee assigned them to a converted pig sty.

Bright Moon slowed her pace, careful not to slosh the bucket. She carried eight precious ladles of soup—thin and a little sour from the rotting onions, but soup all the same. She made her way from the workers' kitchen back to their private "home," praying quietly.

"Jesus, please make this soup worth eating. You know we need our strength." She thought of the letter from Jade, tucked inside her leg wrapping. What terrible news. Outside the camp, people were dying by the thousands! A mysterious epidemic—a sudden and 100 percent fatal disease—had taken almost all their neighboring families. She changed her prayer quickly. "I'm sorry, Lord. Thank you for this soup. Thank you so very much for putting us here and saving our lives."

Bright Moon ducked into the sty and set the bucket of soup down. Two candles burned on an overturned washtub that served for a table. Suddenly she realized how quiet it was. Her six children . . . quiet? Bright Moon quickly glanced around the room. Even in the dim shadows, she could see the fear. It started in their eyes and filled their faces.

"What's the matter?" Her third son was missing. "Where's Sure Hope?"

Kwan emerged from the darkest corner carrying a weak little body. He sat on the washtub, cradling his son.

"He has all the symptoms." Kwan's voice came out a hoarse whisper.

"Is he going to die, Mama?" Little Swan wrapped herself around Bright Moon's leg.

"When did this happen?" Bright Moon ripped Jade's letter from her pant-leg. What did it say? After vomiting, the victim had how many minutes to live? "When?" She knew she must be screaming, but her voice seemed to come from far away. She could only hear the blood pounding in her ears.

"It doesn't matter." Gently, Kwan reached out one arm and took the letter from her. "There's nothing we can do. Except pray."

"Of course," Bright Moon mumbled. In a daze, she motioned her children to gather. They knelt beside Sure Hope's limp form and each began to pray.

Minutes dragged by. An hour. Two hours. Sure Hope still lived.

"Lights out!" The patrol passed by. Bright Moon blew out the candles and they sat in blackness, drawing each breath in unison with Sure Hope. Eventually, the children fell asleep.

Sometime just before dawn, Sure Hope lifted his head. Kwan jerked, instantly awake, and kicked Bright Moon's foot.

"Look!"

"He's alive!" Bright Moon brushed her hand across her son's brow. "He's going to live!"

With morning, the news spread quickly. As the only one to survive the epidemic disease, Sure Hope woke up to instant celebrity status.

"What did you offer the gods?" an old woman hissed to Bright Moon later that morning, leaning toward her at the compost cart. "Please! I must know." Her thin fingers wrapped around Bright Moon's forearm with the strength of a hawk's claw.

Startled, Bright Moon stammered. "Nothing . . . it's not . . . my God's not like that."

"Impossible! When did a god ever do something for nothing?" Her eyes bored into Bright Moon. "You're lying! Why won't you tell me? I have a message from my daughter." Her hand squeezed harder. "Please . . . all but one of my grandchildren are dead. We've offered everything. There is only one son left."

A young patrol girl marched up. "What are you jabbering about, old fool? Do you expect us to feed you for talking? Get back to work."

The grandmother spat at the ground just as she passed. "Dung heap! The Party says there are no gods or spirits. Who's the fool?" Her eyes narrowed and she grabbed the front of Bright Moon's shirt, pulling her close. "Something cured your son, ah? Be kind and tell this old woman."

Bright Moon whispered a silent prayer and abruptly tipped the back end of the cart. Manure slopped to the ground.

"Ai-yah! Now we have to shovel it back up, don't we Grandmother? This is going to take a long time." She wagged her head at the stooped figure beside her, motioning for her to come closer. "Help me and I'll tell you about Jesus while we work."

The old woman grunted. "Jesus? Can't you tell me without killing me? This is heavy work for an old woman."

"Your burden will get lighter." Bright Moon smiled and threw her weight against her shovel. "Trust me."

Bright Moon's next letter from Jade arrived in code. She sat with Kwan, long after the children were asleep, trying to glean every bit of information from her cryptic message.

"What's she talking about?" Kwan's fingers, cracked and marbled by ground-in dirt, traced down the column of characters. "Visitors stole the chicken last night. Who's the chicken?"

Bright Moon took Kwan's hand and whispered, "Old Teacher. He still had a chicken when . . ."

Kwan interrupted. "He was just an old man! A kind old man. I don't understand."

"He was an educated man. Educated by foreign missionaries. Look, Kwan." She jutted her chin toward the letter. She could not bring herself to touch it. Its words crawled up and down the page like rows of marching spiders, a military tactic that threatened any sense of safety she had left.

Kwan read standing. "Our last guest has gone home. We will not see him again until we join him there." He looked at Bright Moon but neither spoke. Finally, he asked the question. "Who was your last guest?"

"Jade's husband." Her eyes focused on a distant point, somewhere only her soul could see. "He's in heaven now." That night, Bright Moon held Kwan tighter than was comfortable.

She woke to a gray sky, blotched with red. Funny . . . she used to enjoy the dawn. Today, she tried to shrink into the quilt, to hide from the encroaching light. She prayed, touching each child's sleeping head. Their bodies overlapped and twisted in baffling directions on the family bed. *How can children sleep like that,* she wondered, *so heedless of cold or cramping?* She quickly prayed that God would keep them in this mysterious contentment, then lifted herself noiselessly over the tumble of arms and legs and onto the damp floor.

Kwan was already up. Bright Moon spotted him through the open door, shivering, his feet warming dark blotches into the frost-covered mud. His head turned one way, then the other. He was looking for something, or someone. He turned around and ripped a sheet of paper from the door, crushing it with both hands.

"Husband!" Bright Moon whispered as loudly as she dared. "Come inside. Are you trying to get sick?" She wanted to know what was in his hand.

Instead of coming in, Kwan twisted and pulled at the wadded ball. Smoothing it just enough to decipher, he held it up for Bright Moon to see. She didn't need to read much to know what the rest said; the standard charges of the revolution were already cliches. "Running dogs of the Americans!" She looked away, signaling that he should get rid of the damning paper before their children woke up. Kwan headed for the designated field where prisoners were to relieve themselves, notice in hand. She had to smile.

Before Kwan could get back, the committee came. They stomped the ground into slush like hungry buffalo and breathed heavily into cupped hands, hot breath venting through their fingers.

"Li Kwan Shin, you are under arrest," the leader shrilled, "for crimes against the people! You will come at once to the commander's office to begin your trial."

Bright Moon blocked the doorway. "He's not here." She tried to keep her voice calm.

"Where has he run to? He will never get away!"

Sticks appeared in the hands of the fidgety cadres. A small crowd gathered, gawking and pecking at the perimeter, trying to scavenge a tidbit of excitement.

"He hasn't run anywhere. Why should he? He's simply putting your limited paper supply to good use."

The leader's snapping-turtle face shut down. Before he could reengage his tripped-up thoughts, Kwan returned.

"Li Kwan Shin, you are under arrest for crimes against the people! You will come at once to the commander's office to begin your trial." The leader took obvious pleasure in repeating his well-rehearsed line. Bright Moon despised him for this.

Kwan and Bright Moon knew this day would come. Long ago, they had memorized the scripture about how Jesus "entrusted his soul to a faithful Creator" as he went to the cross. They had talked about how they would respond.

Kwan answered simply. "I am coming. But, respectfully I ask, may I see my children?"

The committee members fidgeted. No one wanted the on-lookers to see them tear a father from his crying children. Better to go while they slept.

"No! When the Party issues an order, you must obey at once!" The leader brandished his stick like a man threatening a stray dog.

Kwan looked at Bright Moon and forced a smile. Then the committee closed around him . . . then the crowd. A straggler at the edge turned to Bright Moon.

"You're as guilty as he is! I've heard you trying to spread the foreign religion. I've heard you!"

Bright Moon shivered and quickly ducked inside. *What now, Lord?*

Kwan's trial could only have taken minutes. Before she even had the younger children dressed, they were back. This time the straggler led, bowing and babbling to the committee leader as he pointed at Bright Moon. Behind them she could see Kwan, bracing himself on the lurching bed of a manure cart. The crowd spilled around him on both sides like rushing water parted by a river rock.

"She's the one! She's the one!" Bright Moon searched out the piercing voice and recognized the old woman, the one with the iron claws. "Lies and foreign propaganda! She's a spy!"

Bright Moon was confused. Hadn't this old woman gladly listened to the good news of Jesus? Didn't she also loathe the Communist Party? She searched the old, lined face, now animated and flushed with excitement.

The crone caught her questioning stare and muttered, "My grandson is alive . . ."

Bright Moon was even more confused.

"But I'll never see him if they keep *me* here."

Now she understood. She scanned the crowd. Everybody had their own interests to look after. What hope did they have apart from proving themselves to be "reformed" thinkers? Any campaign would receive their desperate support.

A dozen hands shoved her into the cart next to Kwan. Two men held placards, rough wood with a loop of rope at one end. The painted characters announced "Running dogs of the Americans." Someone cracked a whip that snapped across their backs. Together, they lowered their heads and the placards dropped around their necks. The cart bounced forward, throwing them against the sideboards. Manure streaked their clothes and hands as they struggled to stay upright and maintain some dignity.

Mercifully, they didn't go far. The stench was bringing Bright Moon's stomach into her throat. At the central compound the committee stopped and herded the two of them onto a bamboo scaffolding. With a few planks thrown across the top, it formed a crudely built stage that swayed and strained under the burden of two adult bodies.

As the commander of Number Two Farm strutted back and forth below them, he screamed for their confessions. Occasionally, it pleased him to strike them with his bamboo stick. Meanwhile, the crowd surged around them, many trying to show their zeal by throwing rocks and clods of dirt. Finally, the ordeal ended. Bright Moon wasn't sure if it was because the commander was satisfied that enough humiliation had been inflicted or because he was frustrated at the lack of results. They would not confess. Jesus was not some fantastic foreign lie, devised to manipulate the Chinese. He was Truth!

The mass "criticism rallies" continued daily. Guards slept outside their living quarters each night and herded them to the compound each afternoon. The rallies usually included physical as well as verbal torment. Nothing changed for a month, except that Bright Moon and Kwan grew weaker with exhaustion. Then, one day, they took Kwan away.

Every day Bright Moon thanked God for her eldest son, now a young man. Strong Heart remembered his father well and tried to fill his shoes by taking responsibility for his younger siblings. Bright Moon's heart ached once more for her husband. It comforted her to see Kwan's same twinkling eyes and strong cheekbones in her son's face.

This evening, she could pick out his dark frame from among the other workers as they returned from the rice paddies. She watched as he approached the guard shack. Another dark figure appeared. Bright Moon squinted her eyes, trying to improve her eyesight. The man in the shadows handed something to her son. He stood still, but lifted his head in her direction.

She felt her heart beginning to pound. It had to be news of Kwan? Why wasn't her son running? "Hurry, hurry!" she wanted to scream. This was all wrong. He should be running . . . he should be smiling . . .

That night Bright Moon could not speak. Mechanically, she served the family rations. Empty and numb, she watched her family grind through their routines. Strong Heart did his best to break the news. Kwan was dead.

Strong Heart was trying not to shout, but the urgency in his voice rose to a high pitch. "I want to know the truth about my father! I want to know the truth!"

"It won't change anything. And you could get in trouble." Bright Moon pleaded but knew it was useless. "The family needs you. Please . . . please let it go."

The notice declared Kwan's official cause of death: "Lung cancer." They both knew it to be a lie. Kwan had always been healthy. In the last year, during a few allowed visits, Kwan had never complained of illness. But then, he had never complained about anything. He thought always of protecting the children, protecting their hearts and protecting their attitudes. He taught them to be grateful for all things.

"I've already made arrangements." Her son's voice brought her back from her reflections. "A fellow prisoner was released yesterday. He knew Father."

"Why is he talking to you?"

"It's simple. He needs my jacket. I want his information."

Bright Moon watched her son slip out the door and into the blackness.

Bright Moon did not sleep. At the door's first creak, she jumped from the bed. Strong Heart quickly closed the door behind him, then turned, staring at her with eyes she no longer recognized. They were hard and fixed on something she could not see. She hesitated, then threw her arms around him. She waited for him to speak, but no words came.

Months passed before Strong Heart spoke of his father again. Finally, Bright Moon could not bear the silence or the waiting. Once again she met him returning from the fields.

Bright Moon slipped an arm through his. "My Eldest Son, I understand why you went out that night. You needed to know what happened. I need to know, too. Please," she whispered, "whatever it is, we'll carry the truth together."

His arm stiffened under her touch. They turned and followed the raised mud path that bordered the rice paddy. The long way around gave them privacy.

"This is not something you should know."

"You're wrong. I should know. I have a right to know. And you need to tell me." Bright Moon did not feel as brave as her words sounded, but she could not stand to see her son suffering alone.

Strong Heart stopped. "They killed him."

This much she had assumed. She kept walking, saying nothing.

"Several people were questioning him. They had iron hammers. They beat his chest with the hammers."

Bright Moon closed her eyes. *No, Lord, I do not want to imagine this.* She was shaking. Her son continued, tears now streaming down his face. His words spilled and stumbled from his heart.

"Finally . . . they didn't stop . . . until finally . . . finally his lungs ruptured . . . they didn't stop. The prisoner I spoke with . . . he had to clean it up . . . all the blood. They wouldn't let him see a doctor. A month later . . . that's when he died."

She wanted to vomit. She wanted to scream. She wanted to pick up a hammer and lunge for the uniformed cadre that strode toward them now, gesturing for them to hurry up. But she was so dizzy . . . and so weak. The cadre needed to check in Strong Heart's hoe, storing it with other communal supplies. His impatient cursing carried across the glassy smooth water of the rice paddy.

That water was beautiful. The setting sun filled it with streaks and swirls of heavenly color. *I'll go there*, she thought, *it's so beautiful*.

Strong Heart caught her limp body. Leaving the hoe, he carried his mother toward the gate. He scowled at the supply clerk, who immediately fell silent.

Night had fallen long ago. Bright Moon could not close her eyes without picturing Kwan being tortured, so she paced the roadway, looping the compound several times. The guards left her alone—a crazy, wailing madwoman. Whenever she passed, she spat in their direction. They laughed and shrugged their shoulders at some gibberish about "God's judgment."

Bright Moon screamed at the stars. *Was God listening?* "You promised justice! Can't you see them? Murderers! Liars! They're wicked and cruel!" Her cries were choked by her own sobbing. "Why didn't you stop them . . . why didn't you?"

She had never felt such consuming rage. It rolled over her, churning and drowning her in its depths. She could feel the blackness sucking and pulling her soul. Chains of hatred tightened around her heart.

Morning dawned but Bright Moon didn't notice. By now she had stumbled her way across miles of countryside. Day passed into another night. Night passed into another day. She could not stop walking . . . walking. Was she really going mad? Putting one foot in front of the other seemed to keep her mind from slipping away.

Deep inside her spirit she could hear God speaking. He walked with her. Through three more nights and days she continued without sleep or food, crying out to her Lord, and listening.

"Free me, Jesus, from this anger. Rescue me! I hate them and I don't know how to forgive. I don't know how . . ." Her tears became tears of frustration.

She knew her Lord was telling her to forgive. *How could he ask this of her?* Yet she knew he only spoke the truth. It was the only way of deliverance. If she could not forgive, how could she live?

The blackness that engulfed her—it pulled her away from *Jesus*. She could not bear that. She had lost Kwan, at least for this lifetime; she did not want to lose her Lord.

"I want to obey you, Jesus," she wept. "I want to be near you. Please don't let anything separate me from you. Take this hatred from my heart. Help me!"

Bright Moon slumped, exhausted, to the roadside. She lay propped against a boulder, baked by the afternoon sun. Heat transferred into her body from the warm granite. She closed her eyes.

She saw Jesus, stripped, humiliated and pierced, his flesh torn, his face pummeled into an unrecognizable mass, his brow lacerated by deeply embedded thorns. Blood flowed fresh with each beat of his straining heart, running over the iron nails hammered into his wrists and feet.

"Father, forgive them. They know not what they do."

Suddenly, she was part of the crowd gathered on that hill. Her eyes met with his and she knew he was forgiving her. She had put him on that cross. And still he forgave her!

Grace flooded her soul. She laughed when she realized she was crying again. Could there be any more tears? But this was like a cleansing rain. Gratitude mingled with repentance flowed from her deepest being. As the love of God poured into her, she felt that same love surging against her chains of anger and hatred, until they broke away. She was free!

Before long, Bright Moon thought of the long way home . . . her children . . . the old woman who needed to know, just like she did, about God's grace. *One more walk, Lord. Walk me home.* Bright Moon quickened her step.

EPILOGUE

The authorities released Bright Moon from labor camp at age 50, when deteriorating health finally left her unfit for farm work. She now lives with her youngest son. She has dedicated her life, for the past fifteen years, to traveling the countryside, encouraging fellow believers in their hardships and struggles. She puts scripture to song and teaches believers to sing!

During our visit with Bright Moon, she shared two of her favorite songs. You will recognize them as scripture.

For though we live in the world,
　　we do not wage war as the world does.
　The weapons we fight with
　　　are not the weapons of the world.
　　On the contrary,
　　　　they have divine power to demolish strongholds.
2 Corinthians 10:3–4

Therefore, since we are surrounded
　by such a great cloud of witnesses,
　　let us throw off everything that hinders
　　and the sin that so easily entangles,
　　and let us run with perseverance
　　　the race marked out for us.
　Let us fix our eyes on Jesus,
　　the author and perfecter of our faith,
　　who for the joy set before him
　　　endured the cross, scorning its shame,
　　　　and sat down at the right hand of the throne of God.
　Consider him who endured
　　such opposition from sinful men,
　　　so that you will not grow weary and lose heart.
Hebrews 12:1–3

2 *Chapter* 貳

THE GIFT OF COURAGE

"I eagerly expect and hope that I will in no way be ashamed, but will have sufficient courage so that now as always Christ will be exalted in my body, whether by life or by death." Phil. 1:20

"So we say with confidence, 'The Lord is my helper; I will not be afraid. What can man do to me?'" Heb. 13:6

MY FRIEND Wes hires mercenary pilots and flies into South Sudan to minister to an intensely persecuted Church where hundreds of thousands have already lost their lives—in the 1990s! Each time he goes, he says good-by to his children knowing it may be the last time they are together this side of heaven.

We may need courage for less-daunting tasks, but we need courage nonetheless. Without it, we quake and tremble every time Satan growls in our direction. "What will people think if I mention Jesus? What will happen if I tell the truth on my tax return?" Courage comes from having an eternal perspective, from knowing the final outcome. What will people think? Forget it—someday every knee will bow and every tongue will confess that Jesus is Lord. What about my financial future? My inheritance is being held for me, unfading and imperishable! If we kept an eternal perspective, we would laugh at most of what seems so frightening today.

By revealing his plan through his Word, God gives us hindsight in the present. This revelation—that everything truly important is secure and divinely protected by God himself—is a gracious gift. *"Even angels long to look into these things."* It is a gift of perspective; it is the gift of courage.

CHOICES

THE ROOM was cold and small. In the center stood one table, one chair, with one sheet of paper and one pen. A hole gaped in the ceiling where an electric wire and light bulb used to hang, evidence of an attempted suicide. Yung Li sat in the chair, his twenty-four hours almost up. In a few minutes the soldiers would be back.

He stared at the blank sheet of paper. It waited for his confession, pure and impartial. Such a clean void, its emptiness was mesmerizing. If only it could stay that way! If only he could erase what was happening and disappear into the innocence of this untouched page.

His hand shook violently as he picked up the fountain pen, so he dropped it back down. As he pushed back his chair, the startling scrape across the cement floor made him jump. He paced in circles around the rough, wooden table. Perspiration soaked his shirt.

Looking down at the paper, he could visualize the words that would determine his future. But then those words faded away and different words came to take their place—different words and a different future. It was all up to him.

Yung Li thought about past honors bestowed on him by his army unit and of his membership in the prestigious China Youth League. How proud he had been to be chosen as one of twenty from his province to attend a prominent military academy. Everyone knew that graduates from this academy were assured of a high rank. His future looked bright!

But two days ago, guards thoroughly searched every cadet's personal belongings. Among Yung Li's things they found a Bible. His superiors were more baffled than angry.

"Why are you so superstitious?" they asked. "How did your thoughts become poisoned? Perhaps it is your family background that exposed you to such imperialistic influences. That must be the answer, for you are such a fine young man."

Yung Li had stood speechless. A part of him wanted to shout, "No! It is not superstition. It is not poison. If you only knew!" But another part could see his recent bride and could hear the softly murmured plans they liked to make in the gentle nights. Every dream lay in the balance now.

"The Party is a tolerant mother," the officer had crooned. "Because of your record, you will be given a chance to admit your error. If you completely and totally renounce your Christianity, you will be allowed to continue with your career. I am sure it will be a brilliant one." Yung Li remembered the officer's smiling, benevolent mask. He didn't need to be told what the alternative was.

Yung Li sat again at the table and repositioned the paper for the hundredth time. His damp fingertips made little round stains on the edges. He could still have his future. He could say anything he wanted. They would accept anything he wrote. Anything. Time was running out.

Closing his eyes and taking a deep breath, Yung Li began to pray. "Jesus," he whispered, "every reasonable thought tells me I should deny you. Otherwise I will lose everything and everyone I have."

Something in the room changed. Yung Li's eyes flew open. No, it looked just the same. But something was different! He felt calm. Memories began to flood his mind. He thought back over the years since he had first begun to carry his secret Bible, of all the times he had waited until no one was around so he could take it out and read. How precious were those times when he knew the God of the entire universe was speaking words of love and faithfulness just to him! He had never been alone.

The truth resonated in Yung Li's heart. Whatever he lost, he had gained Christ! As he picked up the fountain pen, his hands were steady. He smiled to himself and began to write . . .

The officer read the paper. He read it again, still not believing what he saw. His eyes flashed with fury and he slapped the document down on the table in disgust. Yung Li had carefully written three simple lines.

"I was a Christian.
I am a Christian.
I will always be a Christian."

EPILOGUE

After writing his "confession," Yung Li was immediately expelled from the military academy. Sentenced to labor on a farm, he spent the next ten years living under extremely harsh conditions in a remote part of the country. His in-laws forced his wife to divorce him and refused him any contact with his young daughter.

After ten years, the government recognized Yung Li's honesty and exemplary behavior and restored him to rank. But his wife had been institutionalized in a mental sanitarium and had died shortly thereafter. In the midst of this sorrow, however, Yung Li had the joy of seeing his brother accept Christ.

Eventually, Yung Li had to consider his decision to follow the Lord once again. He forfeited his position and rank. Yung Li now ministers as an itinerant preacher in one of the southern provinces. His brother, who also spent more than twenty years in prison for the sake of the gospel, works alongside him. More than most men, he understands the challenge of Joshua's words: "Choose for yourselves this day whom you will serve."

3 *Chapter* 叁

THE GIFT OF MERCY

"If we are faithless, he will remain faithful, for he cannot disown himself." 2 Tim. 2:13

HOW OFTEN God gives us opportunities to stand for him, only to have us back down in fear or crumble under temptation. We will succumb to gloom and despair if we think God's faithfulness to us is predicated upon our faithfulness to him. We readily transfer our human traits onto God and think, "He will not hear me now; I have failed to do my part. Surely God will turn away from me now. After all, I have let him down so miserably."

But God's faithfulness to us is not the result of our behavior. It is a product of his own character. God is faithful to us because he is a faithful Being. God is merciful to us, not because we deserve mercy, but because he is a merciful Being. God's grace toward us emanates from the awesome glory of his holy nature.

MERCY

A BITTER WIND blew down from the Gobi desert and whipped through the useless tatters of Li Shan's worn jacket. He hunched his thin shoulders and huddled a little closer to the mud-brick walls surrounding the courtyard of the Number 26 Detention and Reeducation Camp. He and a handful of other new prisoners waited their turn to face the camp commander. Most of them did not know the reason for their arrest. Some naively thought that once the commander heard them out, they would certainly be released. Li Shan did not know what to expect. He knew the man who commanded this camp and he knew the man hated Christians. He also knew that once, many years ago, they had been friends.

"Gao Li Shan!" A guard shouted his name and grabbed his shoulder. "You're next."

The courtyard was a morass of icy slush and mud. As he worked his way to the door the other prisoners watched him with faint curiosity, but no one made a move to clear a path. There were too few places to stand with dry feet as it was.

Number 26 used to be a school. It was a drab cluster of cement-block structures built with Soviet aid many years before. The Chinese had themselves constructed the walls that once kept children from outside distractions. Now an outer circle of barbed wire and sentry towers ringed the original walls. The only possible distraction came from an occasional voice beyond the wall—a farmer passing too close, a wandering child—but this was rare. No one visited. Political prisoners were pariahs and it was dangerous to appear even curious about anyone sent here. Inside this camp, you were alone.

Li Shan stood, shivering with cold, in what used to be the

reception area. Soldiers lined the walls. A large desk occupied the exact center. There sat Wu Ling, his old friend! The recognition startled him and he wondered if he had gasped his name aloud or simply thought it. His heart pounded.

The commander slowly looked up from his paperwork. With deliberate control, his eyes worked over Li Shan's bedraggled form, beginning with his muddy shoes and finally stopping when he caught the prisoner's own eyes in a chilling stare. His lip curled into a sneer but no words came out, just a faint hiss of air that immediately condensed and spiraled away from his face.

In that instant, all Li Shan's hope dissipated as well. No friendship survived here. He met the commander's gaze and saw only anger—the anger of betrayal. As young men, full of dreams and idealism, they had shared a cause. Now, the commander did not see an old friend before him but a traitor to that cause.

"I suppose you are expecting a special favor?" The flint-like face didn't move but the eyes flashed.

"No. I trust you simply to be fair."

Li Shan struggled to keep his voice steady. What was fair, anyway? The world had gone mad. Rules were made and changed from one day to the next. Vengeance and vented frustrations seemed to be the only accepted rules of law.

"If I were fair, you would be shot! But there would be no satisfaction in that." The commander paused, relishing the tease. "I will be satisfied when you see that you are wrong. Tell me, Gao Li Shan, how long do you think that will take?" The hard face cracked into a twisted smile. "Do you see? I am giving you the chance to determine your own sentence. When you admit that you are wrong, you will be free!"

The offer stunned Li Shan. This was too easy! He would live! He could leave! All he had to do was . . . what was that? Say he was wrong? Well, did it matter? What purpose did it serve to insist on being right? Stammering with intense relief, his words were incoherent.

"Speak up, Comrade Gao!" The commander's voice cut through the dizzy confusion of Li Shan's mind. "You've been given an opportunity to serve your country and redeem yourself. Now . . .

tell your fellow comrades, tell them how foolish you have been. Tell them how you were duped into believing a foreign religion. Tell them what a useless lie it was and how stupid you were to follow this god—what is his name, Jesus?" The commander came around his desk and thrust his face up next to Li Shan's. "Come, Comrade Gao, tell them now." He fluttered his fingers in the air over his head and laughed. "You can be free!" Several other soldiers joined in his laughter.

Suddenly, Li Shan was silent. Jesus. The commander said it with such scorn—Jesus! All around him, the soldiers stepped a little closer. Their curiosity aroused, they watched him, waiting for him to speak. Jesus. What was it about hearing that name? Li Shan's heart raced, but his mind was clear. Of course it mattered what he said!

He looked around the room, truly seeing the soldiers for the first time. Most of them were so young! Yet their faces were already lined with misery—not just the misery of poverty and hardship, but the soul misery of living in a world where no one can be trusted, where each man is profoundly alone. Already they had witnessed too much cruelty, too much hatred. Their eyes, vacant of any real concern, simply hungered for another diversion on this cold winter day in hell.

Yes, Li Shan thought, it did matter what he said. If he denied what he knew to be true, he would be denying to these men the only hope they had.

Li Shan looked into his former friend's face. "Sir, I thank you for your kindness in offering me freedom, but I cannot do what you ask. It is true that I believe in Jesus, the living God. I cannot say that the truth is false."

"Truth?" The commander shouted in fury. "Your truth is nothing but stupid lies! Foreign lies! Superstition taught in order to control and manipulate our people! You are in league with the foreigners and a traitor to your people!"

Li Shan felt such grief. How could this old friend accuse him of being a traitor? Side by side against the Japanese, they had risked their lives many times for the sake of China.

"It is true that I serve God first. I put my trust in God now, not the Party. But I have betrayed no one. Ultimately, I would be betraying you if I did not speak the truth."

"Speak the truth now, then!" the commander raged. "You say you trust in God, not the Party. Did God issue the clothes on your back? Did God give you the ration tickets that put rice in your bowl? You know how it was before Liberation. Now, no one starves in China. Did God do this? No! The Party has saved us! Isn't this the truth?"

"Whether the rice grows or whether there is even air to breathe, it is God who provides."

"So you deny the great work of the Party and our Chairman?" The commander baited him to speak words of undeniable treason. Li Shan knew the penalty—death without recourse. The silence pounded in Li Shan's ears. Finally, he looked into his captor's eyes.

"For each person you say the Party saves, how many are shot?"

A powerful slap staggered Li Shan. In the cold air, it left a burning streak of red across his face. As he steadied himself, he could hear the soldiers murmuring at his insolence.

Slowly and deliberately, the commander walked back around his desk and sat down. His hand trembled slightly as he gripped a pen and slashed his decision onto the paper extracted from Gao Li Shan's file. At last he spoke.

"Comrade Gao, you will not be shot."

The commander picked up his official chop and stamped an ugly, red smear across the bottom of the page. When he looked up, his eyes were fired with hate and determination.

"You will be broken."

For the next two weeks, the commander did everything to keep his word. He gave orders to withhold the meager food allowance normally given to prisoners. Li Shan wore nothing but rags in a cell where gusting, icy winds blew through with almost no restraint. Finally, the guards appeared and half-dragged him, weak and dizzy from hunger, to the commander's private office.

"Come in, come, Comrade Gao." He waved his arms in magnanimous welcome but stayed seated behind his desk. "I am most curious to see just how well your God has provided for you these past few weeks. Please, give a full report." His laughter burst out harsh and loud.

Li Shan didn't know what to say. Where were the bold words he had spoken so brashly just a short time ago? It was hard just to stand. He was so hungry! *Jesus, where are you?* he thought. *Help me to be strong.*

"Let me make a friendly suggestion," the commander's voice broke into Li Shan's thoughts. "We are friends, aren't we?" The voice was now smooth and conciliatory. "Let's forget about this religious nonsense. You can sign a routine confession—just a formality—and it can be just like old times."

Li Shan buckled slightly and caught himself by grabbing the edge of the desk.

"It makes me sad to see my friend in such poor condition." The commander smiled. "Look! I have ordered a special, fragrant soup for you, a large, hot bowl!" The commander snapped his fingers and a soldier entered carrying a bowl brimming with noodles and vegetables, sprinkled with bits of spicy beef. The aroma quickly permeated the room and Li Shan's stomach began a furious growling.

The commander stood and took the food, passing it slowly under Li Shan's chin. The smell alone nearly dropped him to his knees.

"Now, tell me again, Comrade Gao, who provides for you . . . God or the Party?"

Only one word came to Li Shan's mind. *Jesus.* Jesus, the one who gave him life. Jesus, the one who gave him eternity. *Jesus.* He was with him now! The steam settled in teasing little beads of condensation on Li Shan's face.

"I have given my life to Jesus. He provides everything I need."

"Imbecile!"

Suddenly porcelain shattered and scalding broth ran in rivulets down the heavily cracked wall. Li Shan struggled to keep his eyes off the precious noodles, now a muddy sludge on the floor.

"Take him away!"

Another week passed—still no food. Nothing changed except the cold got even colder. Or was he just getting weaker and less able to withstand the cruel gusts that sent ice into his bones? His muscles ached from the strain of shivers that never stopped. Again, the commander sent for Li Shan.

"Come in, come." For a moment, it was as if the previous visit had never happened. The commander was smiling again. "It occurred to me just today, I should see how my friend is doing. Not well, I see. That's too bad. Didn't you say Jesus was going to provide for you?"

"I did say that."

"Yes, yes. Well, I've taken the liberty of giving him a little help."

The commander nodded towards the doorway. To Li Shan's blurred, watering eyes, a coat seemed to glide on its own into the room. Billows of thickly padded cotton smothered the tiny village seamstress who carried it. Gently, the commander lifted the coat and floated it down around Li Shan's shoulders, surrounding him in a warm cloud.

"You see, Comrade Gao, there really is no God after all, is there? This coat is provided by the Party. Simply admit your error," he paused, "and accept the coat as a token of forgiveness."

Li Shan closed his eyes. Why didn't the coat feel good anymore? It became something dark and heavy, pushing him down. It pushed on his heart; he struggled to breathe.

"No!" he blurted. "I will trust Jesus to provide whatever I need." As Li Shan expected, the commander tore the coat away.

"Guards!"

Several men ran into the room.

"Strip him!"

This was not expected. Li Shan stood in a daze as his few tattered pieces of clothing were ripped from his body.

"Let's see if your God thinks you need anything!" The commander continued to bark angry orders. Soon, the guards bound Li Shan's hands tightly behind his back with a cable of thin wire that cut into his skin with every flinch or shiver of cold.

"Life or death," the commander sneered, "it has nothing to do with an imaginary God. Trust me, Gao Li Shan, eventually you will cry out for help, not to God, but to the Party."

Li Shan lay, naked and bound, on the frozen floor of a corrugated-tin tool shed. He had never known such desolation and mind-breaking misery. Yesterday they had brought him here . . . was it yesterday? Pain from the bands around his wrists and ankles, wrenched together behind his back, consumed his conscious mind. The cold would kill him soon, but not soon enough. One thing he knew; he could not take any more.

Where was God? Where was he? Damn it, where was he? How could God abandon him now? Didn't he care? Didn't he know what was happening to him? God had left him playing the fool, a pathetic fool.

Sobs tore through Li Shan's stiff, contracted body like shock waves. Bitter, angry tears spilled, then froze on his face. He didn't weep because of the pain, or the hunger, or even the cold. He wept for the deadness he felt in his heart. God had failed him. He had lost everything. Li Shan was broken.

When the tears subsided, he mustered what strength he could. "Guard!" He could hear the steps of the patrol outside and shouted again, "Guard!" In his mind, Li Shan rehearsed what he would say as soon as the guard opened the door. He would renounce his faith, renounce Jesus, the sooner the better. As the footsteps came closer, he got ready to cry out again.

The words never left Li Shan's mouth. The steel bands that gripped his flesh suddenly snapped and dropped away! Warmth and strength flooded his body. The pain vanished. The presence of God filled the little shed. An instant later, the shed door crashed open.

"So, the crazy fool is finally ready to . . ." The guard choked on his own laughter. The prisoner that should be dead was standing—strong and free! What strange power did this man have? Struck with terror, he braced himself for an attack.

But instead, Li Shan sank to his knees, oblivious of the guard. What love God had shown him! Even in failure, in his hour of betrayal, God had come. There was no anger. Just mercy. New tears began to flow.

The guard didn't know what to make of this man, weeping prostrate before him, so he fled. News spread quickly through the camp that Gao Li Shan's God had indeed delivered him. Those who overcame their fear tried to get close enough to him to ask questions. The story caused excitement, unrest, then turmoil. Soon, the commander did the only thing he could to maintain control—he released the prisoner.

EPILOGUE

Today, Gao Li Shan pastors a network of underground house churches. He is watched and interrogated regularly, forbidden to see foreigners.

Months after I made contact through mutual friends, the night in which I was to meet Gao Li Shan arrived. But, my companion and I were not sure how to get to his house without being noticed. We left the hotel still wondering what God was going to do and headed for the point where our guide waited.

The power went out! A complete blackout—perfect for hiding two white faces—fell over the city. Silently, we followed our guide's flickering candle throught the dark streets, then up a narrow stairway.

Sitting at a low table in the dancing shadows, Gao Li Shan spoke in a hushed but passionate voice. At first, he was reluctant to tell his story, fearful that I would make him out to be a hero. "This is not about me," he kept saying. "I failed completely. I only tell this to glorify God . . . because of his great mercy!"

4 *Chapter* 肆

THE GIFT OF JOY

"Though you have not seen him, you love him; and even though you do not see him now, you believe in him and are filled with an inexpressible and glorious joy." 1 Peter 1:8

"But I trust in your unfailing love; my heart rejoices in your salvation." Psalm 13:5

EVERY CHRISTIAN knows we are *supposed* to have joy. Therefore, when we don't have joy, we feel left out or overlooked by God. Like the person looking for beef in the old hamburger commercial, we ask "Where's the joy?"

That's a good question to ask. Knowing where to look is key to finding anything, right? At Christmas time there may be a pile of presents under the tree, but a child searching in the kitchen will be disappointed and frustrated.

Peter tells me that joy is the result of knowing what Jesus has done for me (1 Peter 1:3–6). It is the result of beholding his love for me on the cross; of understanding the salvation he has worked for me, the inheritance he has secured for me.

We have so many books about discovering joy. Christians use language that betrays a view that joy is elusive or fragile.

"I've lost my joy."

"Don't let anyone steal your joy."

God desires joy to be a permanent attribute of our lives. It is not a cleverly hidden gift, designed to frustrate us or elude us. He's told us exactly where to look.

Joy is one of those gifts that can be found only under the tree—the tree of Calvary.

CONFORMED TO HIS DEATH

• 1951 •

MRS. TANG MEI-LING hesitated before filling in the blank. Religion? What business was it of theirs anyway? These new Communist Party cadres were becoming as intrusive as the Japanese. *Well*, she mused, *at least they are our own people*. How she had hated the years of Japanese occupation! Anything would be better than the humiliation of foreign rule.

Now the Liberators wanted everyone to register. As a good, patriotic Chinese, she accepted that. But what should she put down? Her parents, grandparents, and great-grandparents had followed Christ. She had grown up in church—even worked for a Western missionary. But it didn't seem very real to her. Were these Christian beliefs her own beliefs? Or were they just a family tradition? It doesn't matter, she finally decided. Resolutely, she filled in the blank. "Christian." She was Chinese, after all. And no Chinese shamed the family. It was her proper duty to show respect for her parents' teaching.

The following days passed into months. She performed well at her job, pushing herself to a place of prominence and recognition. Her prestigious degrees in research chemistry were well known and she held a respected position at the hospital laboratory. She fantasized about achieving great things someday—maybe even the Nobel Prize! Her husband's career as a doctor also showed great promise. Who needed God? She would not deny her "faith" but she certainly didn't need to pursue it.

"Mei-ling, I need to talk to you." Her husband's voice startled her. Mei-ling dropped the armload of books she brought home with her every night from work.

"Chu-sun! What are you trying to do? Scare me to death?" Her eyes adjusted to the dim, evening light of their small apartment. Their electrical ration allowed only one 40-watt bulb and it did little more than attract mosquitoes.

"I'm sorry. I just thought you should know first. I've decided to be baptized as a Christian."

Abruptly, Mei-ling stopped picking up her books. "What? You're getting baptized now? Why didn't you do it before Liberation? You had so many chances. Years! But you refused. Now you want to be baptized."

Mei-ling could feel the rage welling up inside her. Her stomach knotted and churned. She had been studying hard to pass an exam that would qualify her for a foreign research fellowship. If her husband did this foolish thing, it would certainly draw attention to their file—just when it seemed no one remembered she was a registered Christian.

Chu-sun quietly began to stack her books into a neat pile. His face was sober but Mei-ling saw a new brightness in his eyes.

"It never meant anything to me before. I prayed with your father only because he refused to consent to our marriage unless I was a Christian. But now . . . something tells me this is important. I must decide who I am."

Mei-ling clutched the biochemistry text to stop the trembling in her hands.

"You know what this means. Our careers are over. Everything I've wanted . . . the best education, to achieve something important in my field . . . it's finished. And for what? Surely God knows if you believe in him. Why do you need to announce it to everyone else?"

Chu-sun pried her hands off the book and cupped them gently in his own large hands. He answered slowly.

"If we are unwilling to pay a cost, then we are announcing that salvation is worth nothing."

· 1964 ·

Tang Mei-ling glared at the bandages on her smashed leg. *I should be grateful to be alive, I suppose.* But she could not dispel the frustration and anger inside. Once again, her life had been knocked off track—this time by a speeding taxi driver.

For a few brief years after her husband's baptism, Mei-ling had joined him in seeking to follow Jesus. They went to church and patiently accepted the consequences. As expected, her advanced studies were terminated. They lost their envied positions at the hospital and were assigned to routine lab work. But in time, Mei-ling grew resentful and saw her life stagnating when it could have been advancing. After all, her superiors knew her background and talents. Why should it all be wasted?

Secretly she had welcomed the shutdown of all churches in 1958. It gave her an excuse to quietly tuck away her religion and get on with proving herself once again to her local Party boss. She was as loyal and committed to her country as anyone. When her Christian parents emigrated to Hong Kong, she felt relieved from her duty to please them. Her future could only get better, she thought.

"Mei-ling!" Her brother bounded into the hospital room. "We were so worried! I'm so relieved to see you awake. How do you feel?"

"Watch out! Don't bump the bed."

"Sorry. Here, I brought you sweet bean cakes. They're not the best but at least it's better than the swill you're getting here."

Realizing her own rudeness, Mei-ling struggled with a smile. "Thank you, Hong. Thanks for coming." She looked for a chair to invite him to but could only see a chamber pot. Other than that, the room offered only her bed and a broken electric fan. "Well, I'd invite you to sit, but that wouldn't be a very pleasant sight," she laughed. "Here, sit by my head." Wincing, she shifted her upper body to the side.

Her brother eased himself down beside her. "They should let Chu-sun treat you. He's the best doctor here."

"I know. But you know how it is." Bitterness put a strain in her voice. "My doctor's a medical idiot, but his political philosophy is flawless. Chu-sun will mop the lab floor until he learns that loving Mao will get him further than loving religion."

Hong's eyes clouded. "You know it's not religion we love."

"Then what is it? Where is God, anyway? I sacrificed every-thing to remain faithful. It got me nothing. Now it doesn't matter how hard I work, they are still suspicious. They will never trust me. They will never rehire me."

"Rehire you?" Hong looked puzzled.

"Oh, you didn't hear?" Mei-ling's laugh came out harsh and abrupt. "They questioned me during the Four Clearance Move-ment. Mostly about when I helped the American missionaries before Liberation. I was completely honest. I thought God would bless me if I was brave." Mei-ling waved her hand in disgust at her broken leg. "Instead, I was fired . . . and now this. It will take a miracle for this mess to heal properly. Is this a 'blessing'?"

"Maybe it is," Hong whispered. There was no reason to talk louder than necessary, especially with opportunistic ears around every corner. "Here, I have a letter from Father."

Mei-ling's eyes widened. "What! Has it been opened?"

Hong shrugged. "Most likely."

Mei-ling groaned. "Great. Well, you might as well read it to me. But then tear it up and throw it away."

"You read it." The crisp, rice-paper sheet floated to her lap. The neat, vertical rows of characters reflected her father's precise, orderly personality. Suddenly she missed him so much! He could make sense of all this for her!

The letter was short and simple—and dangerous. "We love you," she read, "and we are praying for you."

Mei-ling's eyes filled with tears. "Oh, Father, you don't give up, do you?" Her words were mumbled, soft and forlorn. "I wish we'd gone to Hong Kong with you when we had the chance. Maybe . . . if we had . . ."

Hong put his arms around his little sister. "I'm praying for you too. I'm praying that you'll realize how much God has been with you. How did you avoid being purged in '58? With your back-ground! You have family members that left the country, you and your husband are registered Christians, you even have a history of helping foreigners! Don't you see how God must have protected you? God must have some good reason for keeping you around!" He laughed and headed for door. "I've got to go. I'm late for my mandatory 'Correct Social and Political Thinking' class." He rolled his eyes.

Long after Hong's visit, Mei-ling pondered his words. Had God preserved her? She had always attributed her freedom to her own cleverness and impeccable character. What could they accuse her of anyway? But now she realized how blind she had been—deliberately blind. Many people more clever, more honest, more loyal than she had been shot or sent to prison. How naive to think she had escaped on her own merits. God must have been with her all along!

A year and a half went by before Mei-ling left the hospital. Hong had brought her a Bible and she spent the time becoming acquainted with God again. Her poorly treated leg never fully recovered—the pain was constant—but she could walk with a cane.

Chu-sun came with their two daughters to pick her up.

"Ma-ma! Ma-ma!" It was so good to be with her family again! So good to be going home! Her children flung themselves at her neck and covered her with kisses. A thousand times Chu-sun yelled over their squeals, "Watch Ma-ma's leg!" But no one could stop their laughing.

• 1966 •

Mao's "23 Instructions" lay scattered on the kitchen table. Mei-ling and Chu-sun went back to washing rice and tending the small coal-burning stove. They had nothing to worry about. Confidant, almost smug, they assured each other that they were not in violation of any item on the list.

Mei-ling jumped at the sharp, insistent pounding at their apartment door. They still lived in the hospital staff housing unit and knew all the neighbors. Loud voices in the hallway demanded entrance. Who would come this late at night and so rudely? Her stomach went sour. It could only be one thing. Purge!

Frantic with dread, she gathered her children and pushed them into the corner of the family's one large tatami-mat bed. Throwing a billowy quilt over them, she ordered the girls to stay silent and hidden. There was no point in trying to hide them, she knew, but she did not want them to witness what might happen to her and Chu-sun.

Chu-sun opened the door. There were about twenty of them. Red Guards, they had been fanned into a zealous frenzy by the rhetoric of the leader.

"Eliminate all enemies of the revolution! Clear out all imperialistic poison that oppresses the people! Make way for a new and glorious future!" shouted one of them.

Mei-ling flew from the bedroom at the sound of this familiar voice. Jin-lan! Her old lab partner and dear colleague would surely relent when he saw who she was. But Jin-lan's icy stare showed no trace of friendship.

"Start searching!"

The mob of young people tore through their belongings like hungry dogs in a garbage cart. Mei-ling turned her face away in disgust and grief. For years, she had collected Chinese paintings and antiques with whatever money she could scrimp. She took pride in owning these objects of grace and beauty when the world seemed so filled with ugliness.

"What's this?" A boy barely past puberty sneered at a scroll painting of the Emperor's court. "Does the lab rat wish to be under the thumb of elitist swine again?" Mei-ling saw her kitchen knife flash in his hands, then rip through the heart of her treasured scroll. She bit down on her tongue. If she cried out or objected in any way, things could get worse . . . much worse.

The rampage continued until their furniture was reduced to kindling. Her mother's rice-pattern china set lay in thousands of tiny shards, glittering on the stone floor. Finally, their books— classic literature, medical books, the Bibles—all were gathered into a heap. On top of the books went their family photos and college diplomas.

Chu-sun grabbed Jin-lan's arm. "What are you thinking? You'll burn the building down!"

From behind, a chair leg smashed down on Chu-sun's head and he crumpled to the floor. Mei-ling stifled a scream, not wanting to alarm her children. With several vicious kicks, they worked Chu-sun's body into the corner. Blood marked its path.

"Is this necessary?" Mei-ling's choked voice could barely be heard and tears flowed down her cheeks. Someone . . . she couldn't see clearly . . . lit the bonfire.

"You are obviously reactionaries! Now, where are the guns?"

The accusation stunned her. They were mad!

"I don't know what you are talking about!"

"Then why did your family spend so much time with foreigners?" Jin-lan's face twisted into a leer. "Fourth-generation colonial puppet, aren't you?"

"I don't know what . . ." Jin-lan's sharp slap left a stinging welt across her face.

"Shut up! You're working for the Americans to subvert the revolution! Don't lie and it will be easier for you."

"Look all you want. I have nothing to hide." Her voice hissed with indignation. "I have nothing to be ashamed of!"

Her heart pounded. There was something. In the chimney, barely within reach, she had hidden three study Bibles, with concordances and dictionaries, left by her father. This was not casual reading; they marked a serious student of the foreign religion. The punishment would be harsh.

"We'll be back tomorrow!" Jin-lan waved the mob off it's prey. "By the way, if we find those three other Bibles, you will pay!"

Mei-ling's heart seemed to stop and she sucked for air. How did he know about the Bibles? What was she going to do? He was playing with her. Next time, they would find them for sure!

Ashes rose and fell in weightless, idle swirls. Mei-ling just stared at the half-open door, too numb to move. How long ago did they leave? A muffled sob from the bed snapped her mind back to the immediate crisis.

"My babies!" She darted for the quilt, then remembered her husband. "Chu-sun! Don't try to move."

As quickly and gently as she could, she cleaned Chu-sun's bloodied head and back. Finally, when he looked less frightful, she gave her children permission to come out. That night, in grim silence, Mei-ling methodically tore the pages from her father's three Bibles and burned them over the kitchen coals.

Overnight, their life changed. The building's Party cell-group leader came with an eviction notice and, along with a mob of neighbors and co-workers, drove them from the apartment. The family took only what they could grab on a moment's notice. There was nowhere to go except the new quarters assigned to them—the hospital basement.

· 1968 ·

Winter filled every crack and corner of the heatless cellar. Water dripped from exposed pipes, then froze in dark slicks across the floor. They had no electricity or candles, so Mei-ling scavenged bits of broken mirror. If they placed these by the sunken window, they captured precious bits of weak sunlight and cast the stolen rays into their black hole. Mei-ling's daughters spent their days foraging in cinder bins, looking for any unburnt pieces of coal to ease the freezing nights.

This night, the wind seemed to blow especially cold. Mei-ling leaned heavily on her cane, taking great care not to slip on the icy sidewalk. Oh, to get home quickly! She just wanted to get this smell off her hands!

She had a new job now, one that reflected her new status. She cleaned out the university's perpetually clogged toilets. Her supervisor took great delight in forbidding her to wash her hands when the job was done.

"Why should we waste soap on a filthy traitor?" she had screamed.

Not that there was any soap at home either. They had no ration or money for such a luxury. But, at least, in the privacy of her cellar she could rub the feces from her hands and arms with crunchy, clean snow. Mei-ling grimaced at the odor that clung to her body. Tonight she would rub until her skin was red and raw, but felt clean again!

The walk home seemed so far in this wind. Mei-ling paused to rest at a bus-stop bench and massaged her throbbing leg.

Suddenly a small boy raced up to her, spit in her face, and ran off with her cane. Did she know him? Had his mother been a friend in better days?

"No!" She cried out, reaching for the child.

"Down with traitors and enemies of the people!" Mei-ling shuddered at the hatred in such a young voice. Suddenly the boy turned back. "Stinky pig!" Laughter filled the frosty air around her as more children appeared and joined the cruelty. Someone jerked at the thin wool scarf that covered her head. It tore away, leaving a ragged scrap in her hand. More laughter. A small rock glanced off her chin, leaving a trickle of blood behind. An older boy snapped her cane and flung the pieces back at her. Then, as quickly as they appeared, they were gone.

Mei-ling could feel tears freezing on her eyelashes. "Oh, Lord Jesus . . ." No more words would form. She rubbed her aching leg. What hurt more, the leg or the injury to her pride? Sitting there as evening fell, brushing hot tears from her cheeks, an old memory began to stir. What was that song? Something she used to sing in church.

"O sacred Head, now wounded . . . with grief and shame weighed down . . . scornfully surrounded . . . thorns Thine only crown . . ." How did it go? ". . . pale with anguish . . . sore abuse and scorn . . ."

Mei-ling began to sob. Jesus, her dear Lord Jesus, knew what this was all about. Finally, she understood the song. He loved her! He went through this and more—for her!

"Jesus . . ." He was here with her! She could feel his presence, so gentle and loving, soothing every pain in her heart. She began to sing.

"What language shall I borrow, to thank Thee, dearest Friend, for this Thy dying sorrow, Thy pity without end? O make me Thine forever, and should I fainting be, Lord, let me never, never outlive my love to Thee!"

A man hurrying by paused at the sight of a crippled woman singing in the thickening snowfall. He scowled and scurried away, shaking his head.

Mei-ling sang louder. Suddenly, she realized she was smiling. She couldn't stop smiling! Oh, how much it had taken to get her to see! Jesus loved her so much! What else mattered? Grasping hold of the iron fence that lined the road, she worked her way home. Would she clean toilets for Jesus' sake? Gladly!

"Thank you, Lord," she whispered into the night. "Thank you for letting this happen to me so I could understand."

"Mama! Mama! They took him away!"

"When will he come back? I'm scared!"

Chu-sun was gone! Mei-ling groped her way down the cellar stairs, anxious to reach her girls.

"Shh, shh. Don't fret. It's going to be all right."

Mei-ling felt their small hands clutching at her in the darkness. She fumbled for a stub of candle hidden in the pocket of her trousers. Someone had thrown it in the rubbish bin at work. Gathered around the feeble, yellow glow, she could see tear streaks on their soot-dusted faces.

"Be calm." Mei-ling gave her older daughter the bravest smile she could muster. "Jesus is with us, so we don't have to be scared. Tell me exactly what happened."

"They said Papa doesn't deserve to live. They said he doesn't love Chairman Mao."

"Is that true, Mama? Did Papa do something bad?"

Mei-ling wrestled with her answer. It was all so complicated! For many reasons, she and Chu-sun still regarded the Chairman with deep respect. Look at what he had done for China! The nation had its pride back . . . the chronic famines were over . . . How could anyone accuse them of forgetting?

"Mama . . ." The frightened little voice interrupted her thoughts. "Will they shoot Papa?"

"Papa loves a dead man. That's what they said. They were laughing at him, Mama. Jesus isn't dead . . . is he?"

Mei-ling scooped her girls into her lap. "No. Jesus is not dead. In fact, we are going to talk to him right now."

The huddled trio prayed and then Mei-ling sang to them in the flickering light until, at last, they slept from exhaustion.

A few weeks later, the authorities came for Mei-ling. It was an expected event. She had warned her daughters, praying about it often with them. They prayed for courage. She taught them every Scripture verse she could remember. They would have to survive on their own, staying hidden in the cellar as much as possible. She taught them how to stretch their food coupons as far as possible, buying only half-rotten vegetables and using lots of salt. She went without food as much as she could, storing up her coupons for her children. What she didn't tell them was that she didn't expect to live. She wouldn't need her coupons anyway.

For eighteen months, Mei-ling saw no member of her family.

"Tang Mei-ling!" The guard spit out her name and shoved his rifle barrel into her ribs. "It's your turn." He thrust his face up to hers and sneered. "For the people."

She dropped her head, too tired to react. For twenty days the "purging" had continued—one group after another, screaming her crimes, demanding her confession. They came for her at all hours of the day and night to keep her body off schedule and her mind disoriented. The pain in her leg kept her awake. In one session, they had kept her standing for 36 hours. *Oh, just to sleep!*

The guard pushed her into the noon sun, then herded her towards an outdoor platform. A grim, expressionless woman planted herself in Mei-ling's path. She clutched a clipboard filled with papers in one hand and stabbed at the listed rules with the other.

"During your session, you will stay alert! You will listen to your accusers! You will answer truthfully and confess your crimes! If you show true remorse, you might be fortunate and be shown mercy! If you do not, you will be punished in a manner suitable for traitors!" She paused. "You must be an important criminal. Everyone has been ordered to attend this session—more than 2,000."

Mei-ling gasped and jerked her head towards the stage. All her former co-workers crowded the assembly yard. Nurses, doctors, the entire hospital staff, even old professors and classmates attended.

"See what a stubborn nuisance you've become!" The warden screeched and slapped Mei-ling's face. "Today, don't waste everyone's time!"

Mei-ling knew what she meant. They wanted a public confession. She was to be an example. They wanted an intellectual, a religious reactionary, a foreign abetter—she was all those things—to be humbled and beg forgiveness of the Party. And they wanted her to do it front of 2,000 people.

Mei-ling hugged her chest, as if she could still the heart slamming against her ribs. *Where is Chu-sun?* She longed for his reassuring smile. Part of her wanted to race onto the stage and search the crowd for his familiar face. If he was alive, he would be forced to attend. She ached just to know. *Are you alive, my husband?*

Again, she felt a sharp prodding in her ribs. A ladder of bamboo scaffolding rose to the six-foot platform. Barely finding the strength to climb, she reached the top and lifted her eyes to look for Chu-sun. Her name blared from a pair of speakers hoisted up into the branches of a sycamore tree. Instantly the crowd reacted with angry shouting. Some just stared at her, their eyes boring into her with a mix of hatred and curiosity. Again the speakers sputtered and squealed. The woman with the blank face barked out her list of crimes.

They hate me! She couldn't look anymore. The sea of faces, with their mouths moving and fists shaking, terrified her. "*I'm not the enemy!*" she wanted to scream back. She felt her whole body trembling. *Oh, where are you, Chu-sun?* Unable to bear the stares of the crowd, her downcast eyes frantically searched along the front rows trying, at least, to find his shoes.

How long would this go on? The clock on the hospital tower moved from noon to half-past. The scorching sun added to her fatigue. Minutes felt like hours and the crowd grew more enraged with each question.

"Tang Mei-ling! Obviously, you care nothing about your children. If you did, you would confess your crimes. Then you could go home to them. I'm sure they miss you very much."

"Confess! Confess!" The mob roared.

Mei-ling could not control her tears. How could they accuse her of not loving her children? And how cruel to torture her with such false promises!

She was not allowed to close her eyes, so she saw the thick bamboo rod before it hit her. The blow fell across the back of her legs, dropping her to the rough planks of the stage. A second blow fell across her shoulders. Her arms splayed out in an instinctive effort to catch herself and fiery pain knifed through her entire body. Was her shoulder dislocated? Someone in the front row laughed.

"Look at the big shot now. The elitist intellectual studies dung now. Maybe she can give us a lecture."

More jeering erupted from familiar voices and the humiliation roared in Mei-ling's ears. Her mind slipped back to a quieter, safer time. Her mother used to hold her and rock her to sleep with a simple song. "Jesus!" Mei-ling began to sing, her words drowned out by the uproar. "Jesus loves me, this I know . . ." *I have no one else but you*, she thought. *I have nothing but God himself.*

The crowd saw her lips moving and seemed momentarily appeased. She must be confessing. But as the shouts subsided, Mei-ling also stopped singing. She didn't want them to know what she was really saying! The next crime was announced, inciting more hysteria. She began to sing again. "Yes, Jesus loves me . . . yes, Jesus loves me . . ." Again, they assumed she was confessing.

Finally, the time for actual "purging" came.

"Tang Mei-ling, we are giving you the chance to clear your conscience. Tell us exactly how you and the foreign devil spied for the United States."

No words came. She could not lie about the missionary who had come to tell them about Jesus. She could not deny the truth of his message. She had nothing to say.

"Tang Mei-ling! You are protecting an enemy of your people!"

Someone yanked her to her feet. The bamboo rod crashed across her kneecaps and she staggered, grabbing at her accusers to keep from falling. In disgust, they shoved her back to the foot of the stage. The crowd roared in approval.

Exhausted and desperate for escape, Mei-ling prayed silently. *Oh God, let me sleep with my eyes open.* But before even finishing this short prayer, she scoffed at herself. *I must be dreaming if I think God is going to answer such a foolish prayer.* But she knew she must not close her eyes. If she did, they would torture her more to keep her awake.

The crowd drifted silently from the assembly yard. *Where was everyone going?* Mei-ling blinked several times. A strange sensation of relief settled over her. The intense intimidation, the shame—it was all gone. She looked up at the clock tower. Five o'clock! Was it a dream?

"You are free to go." A flat voice broke her daze.

Mei-ling just stared. She pinched herself. Then she rolled her shoulder . . . fine. It was over! It seemed God had answered her wildest prayer! Stumbling through a blur of tears, Mei-ling scrambled down the ladder and raced for home.

Why is that woman staring at me? Mei-ling slowed down, then stopped as if to rest, behind the pump shed. Something told her to wait. Suddenly, the mysterious woman appeared in the shadows next to her.

"You were wonderful! You looked so calm and peaceful, all those hours. Someone said you must be a very well trained spy to be so brave but I think everyone knew you were innocent!" Her face beamed and she took Mei-ling into a vigorous embrace. "I know they are angry with you now, but Jesus must be so proud. God bless you!"

With that, she disappeared.

Mei-ling sat on the edge of her septic pail. So she wasn't crazy! She hadn't just passed out. How gracious of God to let her know he really had answered her cry. Mei-ling grinned and whispered in the direction of the woman's steps, "Thank you."

She had to get back to work. As Mei-ling lifted the heavy pails, she looked up at the hard, gray sky. Inside she felt warm and strong. She whispered again, "Thank you."

EPILOGUE

Mei-ling spent four more years under house arrest in their cellar home. Eventually, Chu-sun was also released.

Inexplicably (this is another story!) in 1979, papers came through and the entire family emigrated to Hong Kong. Today, Dr. and Mrs. Tang and their grown children live in California. Dr. Tang Chu-sun and his daughter, a licensed acupuncturist, frequently travel back to China, encouraging and ministering to fellow believers there.

In a recent visit I had with Mei-ling, she reflected: "We give thanks that God did not bring us out of China earlier, with the rest of my family. If he had, we might not be Christians now. We might love the world more than the Lord. We might have many material possessions but be very poor in spiritual ways. God knows our hearts and he protected us from temptation. He let us experience this suffering that we may know that he is God and cares. He let me experience his presence and really see him. I feel as King Solomon did—I just want this wisdom and nothing else." She paused and smiled. "A millionaire can't have what I have in Christ . . . this joy and peace."

5 Chapter 伍

THE GIFT OF POWER

"I came to you in weakness and fear, and with much trembling. My message and my preaching were not with wise and persuasive words, but with a demonstration of the Spirit's power, so that your faith might not rest on men's wisdom, but on God's power." 1 Cor. 2:3–5

EVERYONE NOTICED, and smelled, the unkempt young man sitting in the front row of our little church. He glared at the pastor through an alcoholic haze. During the message, a few heard him mutter aloud, "Well, God, if you're real, you'll have to show me." The service ended and I met Skitch. His clear eyes sparkled. He waved his hands in the air, rotating his wrists in great excitement. "God healed me!"

As a former world-class skateboard competitor, Skitch had broken his wrists seven times. Severe arthritis held them in a painful lock. He told us about his prayer and how, for the last half hour, his wrists had burned as he felt God's presence on him. Overwhelmed by God's love, he cried unashamed.

Sometimes we forget who needs whom. We labor with the idea that God's kingdom rests on our shoulders. We assume the burden of proof for God's existence, his truth, his power. Have you ever felt reluctant to pray because you didn't want God to look bad if nothing happened?

If God doesn't expect us to carry our own burdens, why do we think we need to carry his? God calls us to be his hands, his feet, his mouthpiece—not because he is helpless without us, but because this is the arena in which we will experience his presence and power. And he knows how greatly we need them both!

"WHAT MANNER OF MAN IS THIS?"

PERSPIRATION soaked through Chin Lai's only good shirt. A cool breeze blew off the Min Jiang River and fog shrouded the ferry landing, blocking the weak, dawn sun. Heat wasn't making him sweat. It was all that money!

"Have you had a good breakfast?"

Mrs. Ma pressed a small, warm bundle into his hands. She had wrapped and knotted a threadbare kitchen towel around a flat tin container. Chin Lai looped his finger through the knot and Mrs. Ma beamed with satisfaction.

"Pickled cabbage, not too sweet, and some boiled duck eggs. My own ducks, you know. The rice is still hot."

"Old Grandmother, you are going to spoil me like a small child. You shouldn't bother." He smiled and patted her arm. "Go home before you catch cold in this wet air."

"You're much too young to tell me what to do," she said, laughing. "I'll spoil you if I want. Besides, you're on a very important mission. You are a representative of God's people and a trusted steward of God's money. I'm just making sure you get a proper send-off."

Suddenly, the quiet riverbank rang with cheerful greetings. "Surprise! Good morning!" Groggy fisherfolk glanced up from their trolling nets as several figures appeared through the mist. A farm woman standing next to Chin Lai with a basket of onions chuckled. "Your friends, ah?" Her gaping mouth displayed crooked teeth blackened by beetlenut juice. "You must be very important . . . and prosperous." She cleared her throat and spat at Chin Lai's feet. "There's no ferry today. Be careful." Hoisting her basket onto her head, she turned to the various boats bobbing along the shore.

"Thanks for your concern, but I've made arrangements with

one of the captains. I'll be fine."

The woman cocked her head. "A private passenger, ah?" Then she quickly disappeared, clucking to herself. "Be careful."

Brother Fan drew close and tugged at Chin Lai's sleeve. "Don't let them sell you old wood. Look for termite droppings."

"And no used nails," Sister Huang added. "No cheap, rusty junk in our church!"

The delegation murmured in agreement. "This is going to be a fine church. A place where everyone can come and be comfortable."

Chin Lai stood taller and squared his shoulders. How proud he was to be so trusted! Or did they trust him? Were they really here to make sure he headed for Fuzhou city and not elsewhere with their money? He brushed the doubt aside and bowed to the group.

"You give me great honor by allowing me to serve you in this way. I assure you, I will find the best building materials your money can . . ."

"Hey, you! Do you want to go somewhere or make speeches?" A foul-smelling sailor interrupted Chin Lai and shoved a grimy hand into his chest. "One yuan or you can swim." He seemed oblivious of anyone else except his paying passenger.

"Ai-yah!" Mrs. Ma protested. "Why do you have to be so rude? Of course he can pay." She glanced at Chin Lai with a slight shake of her head. "Here, I'll pay for him."

The crewman grunted, snatching the money from her hand. "He still needs a wet nurse to stand up for him, does he?" His cackle carried across the water, then broke up into a spasm of coughing. The huddle of well-wishers waited, embarrassed that the farewell party had soured. Finally, the sailor cleared his throat, spit on the dock, and swaggered off to the boat.

Mrs. Ma turned to Chin Lai and murmured, "Whatever you do, don't let them see where you carry your money. There are many pickpockets on these ferries." She squeezed his arm. "God bless you and keep you safe."

Chin Lai wondered at this old widow. She treated him so kindly. Before his friend took him to meet the Christians, he didn't know there were people like this. No one wanted anything to do with an ex-convict, a common thief. But she had welcomed him into her home where the believers met and told him all about a god named Jesus. This true God loved him and had the power to forgive and wash away everything bad he had ever done. They really believed in this forgiveness and accepted him as a new man. It was beyond imagination!

Chin Lai twitched until he could feel the money pouches against his skin. Under his arms, strapped to his thigh . . . they were all there and secure. He wanted to run this errand for the church—to repay their kindness and to prove he was truly a new creature, just like their book said.

The splitting plank creaked and wobbled as Chin Lai made his way on board. The boat was little more than a barge. One central mast held a filthy sail that boasted more patches than original canvas. Eight sailors sat at their oarlocks and oars. Anticipating the work ahead, they had already stripped off their tattered shirts. Sweat rags hung from rope belts around their waists. They glared at Chin Lai.

"Excuse me . . . good morning . . . excuse me . . ." Chin Lai tried not to show his dismay at the sludge swirling around his feet. His new shoes!

"Sit down!"

Where? He didn't dare ask so he just settled on a thick coil of rope in the stern. Too late, he realized it was the anchor rope, still dripping wet.

Chin Lai recognized the second oarsman as the one who had taken his fare from Mrs. Ma. Before he could look away, the sailor caught his eye.

"Please, make yourself comfortable!" He quickly had the attention of the rest of the crew, including the captain who stood with one hand on the mast. Nine pairs of eyes narrowed in on him. "We want our honored passenger to enjoy his journey."

Oars splashed into the water and the boat pulled away from the landing. It was either the snatch of the current or the burst of raucous laughter. Whichever, suddenly Chin Lai felt extremely uncomfortable.

The river grew wider and more deserted as they left the fishing boats behind. They pulled into the deep center where the current could do most of the work, carrying them eastward toward the sea. The crew had only to keep the barge from being pulled onto occasional rocks and into passing debris. As the sun rose higher, tentacles of mist that coiled just above the water's surface warmed into a steaming octopus that wrapped its suffocating arms around each man. Chin Lai wiped his brow with a shirtsleeve.

As he brought his arm down, he noticed the oars had stopped their dip and tug against the pull of the river. The steady banter of the crewmen grew silent. Why was everyone looking at him? That uncomfortable feeling turned into a sick churning in his stomach. Pirates! Did they know about the money? How could they?

Suddenly, several grinning sailors grabbed for his shirt and trousers. The boat rocked dangerously as a rain of wild blows landed on his stomach and back and pitched him to his knees. Chin Lai heard his fine, new cotton clothes ripping in several places just before his head hit the slimy deck. Darkness and searing pain engulfed him. Through the ringing in his ears and his pounding heart, he could hear their voices.

"Ai-yeeh! The river gods are happy with us today!"

"Look! It's a human bank. We're rich!"

"You see? A wife is good for more than one thing after all. Sharp eyes and ears have earned her rice."

Chin Lai could not lift his face out of the puddle being formed by his own blood mixed with water sloshing over the tipping sides. Now he remembered the farm woman with the basket on her head. He could hear her odd chuckling: "Be careful." Chin Lai groaned. Had his head split? Gingerly, he raised trampled fingers to his scalp.

A black, calloused foot pinned his arm to the deck.

"What are we going to do with this piece of garbage?"

"A gift for the river goddess Ma Chu! For her generosity in sending us such good fortune!"

The captain spit in disgust. "You and your idiot superstitions. You have brains like rotten fruit! The Communists will soon be

Meeting us at the home of a mutual friend, Bright Moon records her story.

Shao Lan (center) and her mother (right) are all smiles as they tell of her deliverance from a condition that held her in a suicidal, catatonic state for two years.

Teacher Wu examines the old, cracked pages of a Book of Matthew, hand-stitched into a corrugated cardboard cover. Placed in a rough box and hidden in a shed wall for many years, this portion of Scripture brought revival to an isolated mountain village.

As mentioned in "The Hidden Gospel," Yi tribespeople hike back to their village carrying the first complete Bibles printed in their own language.

Young Christians carried a disposable camera into an area closed to foreigners and brought back this picture of believers building their church.

Believers hold their first meeting in a newly built church. Young and old helped to make the mud bricks used in constructing this building, the finest in the area.

The author with Bao Chen, an itinerant evangelist who spent many years in labor camp, and the woman healed of blindness in the story "Foreign God."

This country woman beams with new-found joy. She traveled a full day to come tell us how Jesus healed her blind eyes and saved her village.

Christians gather for baptism in a remote region off-limits to foreign visitors.

Released after 15 years of forced labor, a pastor teaches one of his many house church flocks.

Those who can't squeeze into a home gathering crowd the tiny courtyard outside.

A home meeting overflows into the center courtyard.

In a small home hung with song charts, house church members receive Communion from their pastor, returned from 20 years of exile in the harsh regions of western China.

Most groups meet without any formally-trained leadership. Believers encourage one another with scripture, prayer and personal testimonies.

Many congregations have no church building and simply meet in courtyards or under the trees.

A cartload of more than 300 Bibles leaves for the train depot. They will be delivered to the Miao tribe where 20,000 Christians have been sharing only 60 Bibles.

In answer to many prayers, the government has approved a Bible School in Kunming, capital of Yunnan Province, for students from the minority tribes. These young women pray for the power of the Holy Spirit before returning to minister in their remote home areas.

Students from several minority groups dress up and join the author in the court-yard of the Kunming Bible School.

Yunnan Province is home to over 24 large minority nationalities, each with its own language, dress and customs. This mother and daughter have come to the city to attend a Christmas service at a newly opened church.

Christians who have been through the worst are the boldest in their faith, no longer fearing what man can do.

A delighted elderly woman proudly shows off her new, large-character Bible, just delivered from outside China.

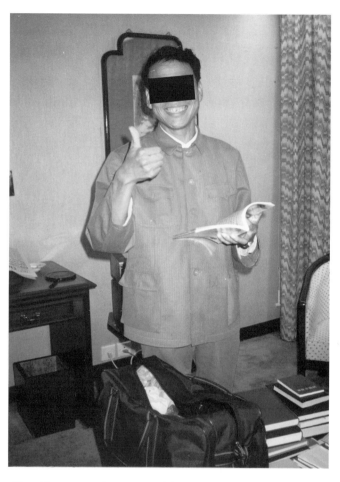

This Christian worker expressed his joy over a recent delivery of Bibles and study materials.

The wife of a martyred pastor cherishes her large-character Bible
from outside China.

After many years of no contact with the West, Chinese bystanders are astonished to hear their language spoken fluently by missionary James Baker, the author's father.

This old Shanghai church was closed by the Communist Party for many years and, like countless others, used for housing and storage. Crowds waited for hours on the day it was reopened in the early '80s. There was standing room only on the Sunday we visited this TSPM-governed church.

As the leaders and crowds left the building, we were moved to see
this unannounced, spontaneous gathering for prayer at the altar.

Two sisters pore over the Scripture. They are responsible for leading several hundreds of believers in their mountain region, where no other pastors are left.

In China's official churches, Bible teaching and baptism are denied to all under age 18. Christian families treasure pictorial Bible story books brought from outside China.

A woman petitions the gods by placing her offering before idols. To fill the spiritual void left by Communist ideology, many in China are returning to ancient practices and ideas.

Intended to frighten off evil spirits, this 10-foot idol looms over the entrance to a Buddhist temple.

Ancestor worship, practiced by Buddhists, often involves burning incense before photos displayed in the family home.

Once banned by the Communist government, idol worship in Buddhist temples is now permitted. Here a child is being taught by parents to bow before an idol.

Prayers and images of "guardian spirits" are pasted on the doorway for protection against evil spirits.

Since the '80s, more relaxed economic policies have allowed individuals to pursue some small-scale free enterprise. Here a street is jammed with vendors selling what they have grown on their own patches of ground.

This old woman has her own business selling boiled pigeon eggs on the street.

This entrepreneur has set up a sidewalk shoe repair shop.

Early mornings and evenings are permeated by the aroma from enterprising sidewalk food vendors.

The ubiquitous presence of The Chairman pervaded China for decades and still dominates Tiananmen Square.

Soldiers relax around the park gate during Lantern Festival in Kunming.

University students along the Shanghai Bund gather around us to chat, eager to practice their English. They welcome the chance to learn about life outside China and frequently ask about faith in God.

This student gives us his address, hoping we can send him literature.

Taking advantage of their one day off, Shanghai's eight million people all seem to have someplace to go on Sunday afternoon.

A young boy smiles for the American's camera. During World War II,
Kunming served as home base to the American volunteer pilots, *The Flying
Tigers*, in the fight against Japan. In this city, I sensed that an attitude of good
will toward Americans still remains, even among the new generation.

A typical city street alive with the clang of bicycle bells, blaring bus horns, and a sea of pedestrians bustling in every direction.

In a country of over 1 billion, manpower is often the most available natural resource.

Tribal people in colorful dress frequently come down to the city of Kunming for supplies, trading and festivals.

Ancient rooftops of a small town. Homes are built around a courtyard, then additions are made as the extended family grows.

Much of rural China has remained structurally unchanged for generations. This narrow road, which winds through Dali in Yunnan Province, is a typical small town thoroughfare.

A woman prepares dinner in a kitchen typical of rural, interior China.

A stroll through the narrow streets of old Kunming at dinner time took us by many fragrant meals being cooked over traditional coal-burning braziers.

Country villages rise up like small islands from a vast sea of rice paddies. Itinerant evangelists, most of them elderly women who survived the Cultural Revolution, visit these far-flung villages which are accessible only by foot.

Cargo and ferry boats of ancient design still ply China's rivers right alongside modern vessels.

School children on a field trip visit the Great Wall.

In the far north, China's Gobi desert is home to minority peoples of cultures very different from the Han Chinese.

Men and women join in the backbreaking work of planting rice seedlings one by one.

A treasured "little emperor" is given the best food and care. China's "one child only" policy has slowed population growth, but has also put severe strains on society.

About 80% of China's 1.3 billion people live and work in the countryside. This young woman has sold her produce at the market and heads home with her purchases.

rid of the likes of you."

For a moment, the celebration chilled. The pirates looked at one another nervously. Out here on the river, it was easy to slip and forget that China's wind had changed. Correct ideology was as important to survival as knowing the idiosyncrasies of the weather. Finally, the captain grabbed an oar and stabbed at the air.

"A curse on all idiots, especially the Red ones!"

He shoved the oar into the chest of the nearest crewman and sent him sprawling across the deck. The tension broke into relieved laughter. But they still had the person of Chin Lai to deal with.

"Over there." The same oarsman that had taken Chin Lai's one yuan fare was now counting his money under the wary scrutiny of every other pirate. He waved a pouch of coins towards the northern bank. "No one ever sails into that cove."

The captain grunted his approval and kicked the toppled crewman back to his feet. "Hurry up . . . all of you. Do it before the patrol boats come."

Chin Lai didn't want to believe what he heard. They were going to kill him and throw him overboard! He could do nothing. Every limb ached from his beating. He thought about the believers, waiting and waiting for his return . . . no word from him . . . their money gone. "Of course they will think I stole it," he moaned to himself. He tried raising himself up by pulling one arm under his body, but another kick quickly dropped him back onto his face.

"Where do you think you're going, Fish Food?" The voice cackled from above the kicking foot. Chin Lai saw a pair of hands pull rope from a bronze, muscular waist and wrap the ends around two gritty, calloused palms. The pirate was going to strangle him. He leaned down until Chin Lai could feel his heavy breath.

Suddenly the pirate's body flew over Chin Lai and landed with a thud, his head hitting an oarlock. "Wah?" he moaned, holding his head in his hands as blood oozed through his fingers.

The boat heaved wildly, knocking several of the crew off their feet. Astonished, they looked out across the river. Windwaves rose and crashed, tossing the barge around like a dry leaf. Dark clouds raced across the sky, gathering in black, ominous billows above their heads. The wind swirled, seeming to change direction with every gust. Water pitched over the sides, sweeping men off their plank seats. They had never seen a storm so sudden and unpredictable! Within moments, sheets of driving rain engulfed the boat, making it impossible to see.

"Watch for the rocks!" a voice screamed.

A blast of wind caught the sail and tore it from the mast. The remnant flapped crazily in the gale.

"Ma Chu, have mercy on us!"

"Shut up, you mewling old woman! Are you a sailor or a superstitious coward?"

But the wind had risen to a howl and drowned out the captain's voice. In terror, the crewmen clutched any piece of boat they could and abandoned all efforts to bail water. The racing current carried them straight for the rocks.

"Throw the money overboard!" Screaming above the wind, a pirate desperately tried to convince his shipmates. "Ma Chu is angry with us!" He lay prostrate on the deck, his arms wrapped tightly around the base of the mast.

"Shut up!" the captain shrieked from his perch at the anchorhold. "You throw one yuan overboard and I'll take it out of your worthless hide. Ma Chu is a fairy tale!"

Chin Lai's face lay close to the hysterical pirate. He tried to make himself heard, crying, "Your captain is right! Ma Chu is no use to you. We need the true God to help us."

The river lifted in rushing eddies as it was forced to divide around the rocks. They felt the boat rise. The crash came an instant later, sending a violent shudder through the hull and through the body of every man on board. The mast gave way at the base, tearing a hole in the deck. Quickly, it disappeared into the river as insignificant as a toothpick. Water poured through the gaping hole. Chin Lai looked for the pirate who had been there a moment earlier. He saw a bloody mass where the flying wood had caught the side of the pirate's face. The man screamed uncontrollably as incoming water swept his helpless body towards the side.

The captain lurched to his feet and tried to make his way forward but was immediately thrown back down. Even in the roar of the storm, everyone could hear ripping boards and shattering beams as the boat began to break up. Chin Lai squinted his eyes, trying to see through the pelting rain. The pirate captain landed beside him, grasping wildly for any handhold. Chin Lai freed one hand and locked his arm over the captain's shoulder. Looking into his face, he saw none of the captain's former arrogance and rage, only a consuming fear.

The captain's hoarse voice rasped into Chin Lai's ear. "You say you know the 'true God.' Then pray to him! Now!"

Startled, Chin Lai hesitated.

"Now! Is your god real or not?"

What could he do but pray? Chin Lai tried to calm his own racing heart enough to form an acceptable prayer. He was such a new Christian! What was he supposed to say? What if nothing happened? The thought of failure was almost as frightening as the storm.

Another voice from the splintering bow interrupted his panic. "Yes, pray to your Christian god! Please!"

Very little of the boat remained above water. All eyes fixed on Chin Lai. No religious words came to mind. He just prayed.

"Jesus, please help us. Save us from this storm."

He had to yell so that the men knew he was praying. Yelling made him sound more confident than he felt. After all, what was he asking?

Suddenly, the wind died. The waves fell. The rain stopped. They drifted in a steady current that bore them gently towards the shore.

If the men feared the storm, they feared this eerie, abrupt change in weather even more. They stared at Chin Lai. Chin Lai stared at the river and the sky. No one spoke.

Finally Chin Lai bowed his head to hide his tears. God had brought a storm and then stopped it—just to save his wretched life! He remembered a story from the Bible that Mrs. Ma had recited in a meeting: "In fear and amazement they asked one another, 'Who is this? He commands even the winds and the waves, and they obey him!'" He felt the same awe and shock. From the stunned look on the pirate's faces, he knew they did too.

A thick, trembling voice broke the silence. "Who is your God?" Chin Lai looked up and locked eyes with the captain.

They hauled what was left of the boat onto the beach, but no one felt like working. Repairs could wait. No one could think of anything except what had just happened on the river, and no one wanted to talk about anything except this unfamiliar, new God named Jesus. They listened to Chin Lai tell them about an all-powerful God who loved them and who allowed himself to be humiliated and killed in order to show that love. This God made the stars and oceans, but heard a poor man's prayer. It sounded so strange . . . but wonderful! That afternoon, as the sun set over the Min Jiang River, a crew of pirates chose to love and serve a new captain—the God Jesus.

The next morning's ferry puttered past a cove harboring a curious group of disheveled men. They appeared in high spirits, considering the condition of their wreckage. One of the men seemed to be teaching a song which the others sang with gusto, sending it far out on the misty river. They sang about something described as "amazing" but the passengers on the ferry couldn't quite catch the rest. "Must be drunk," they muttered to one another, shaking their heads.

EPILOGUE

Chin Lai finally reached Fuzhou and made his purchases. The pirate crew not only had returned every penny of his money, but they then transported his materials, providing safe escort back up the river. To the amazement of every believer, the pirates then stayed and helped to build the church!

6 *Chapter* 陆

THE GIFT OF SOVEREIGN CARE

"Do not withhold your mercy from me, O LORD; may your love and your truth always protect me." Psalm 40:11

"But the Lord is faithful, and he will strengthen and protect you from the evil one." 2 Thess. 3:3

MY THREE-YEAR-OLD has a profound need to be in control. When opposed, she will state with as much authority as she can muster, "I'm the boss!"

Really, there's not much difference between my daughter and the rest of us. We readily lapse into our old nature of defiant little despots trying to usurp the Creator's authority over our lives.

Like my daughter, we do not know the burden of what we want. We cannot foresee the disastrous consequence of getting our own way. When I warn my daughter, she rarely believes me. She declares, "You're mean!" We often feel the same way about God when we chafe against his rule.

I am protecting my daughter from dangers and consequences she is not even aware of. I love her too much to stop protecting her just because she doesn't appreciate my effort. How we must grieve our heavenly Father when we challenge or violate his divine direction. Yet our folly does not diminish his love for us. He continues to guard us from dangers we may never see, to protect us from enemies we may never meet, to shepherd, to discipline, to call us back to himself.

With deep gratitude and relief we should declare, "I'm *not* the boss!"

SHAO LAN

AH MING packed, then unpacked, packed, then unpacked each of her well-worn belongings. Actually, everything fit quite easily into her nylon-net sack, but packing was a delicious ritual to be savored. As a servant girl, she didn't have many opportunities to travel. Travel! What a wonderful word, filled with anticipation and adventure, even though she was only going home. The endless packing also helped Ah Ming to ignore the guilt she felt over leaving her young mistress behind.

She glanced over to the far corner of their tiny room where Shao Lan lay in a tight curl. Her drooping face, damp with sweat and neglected spittle, lay in the shadowy cocoon woven by her thin arms and legs. A fly droned around her ear, landing with brazen liberty until Ah Ming defended her mistress with the snap of a ragged shirt. Ah Ming sighed. Would Shao Lan really be all right for a week without her?

Shao Lan was fourteen now. Ah Ming remembered coming to the Li household one year ago, listening as Li Tai-tai described a bright, beautiful daughter to her—the daughter she once had. "The doctors can find nothing physically wrong with her," she explained. Yet Shao Lan lived in a wordless stupor. Sometimes she would cry for hours, or just lie on her bed, listless as the buoys that floated far outside the Shanghai harbor, drifting in the fog. At twelve years of age, a mysterious fog had come and, in effect, had swallowed everything up—her family, her friends, her studies. Ah Ming remembered the mother's words, heavy and slow, as she recounted Shao Lan's many suicide attempts. And finally, weeping, she had told of putting Shao Lan into the provincial mental hospital.

But now you have me, Ah Ming thought with gentle satisfaction. *I take much better care of you, don't I?* She didn't blame Shao Lan's parents for taking her out of the hospital. One year there had turned her into a spastic, shock-damaged child, helpless as an infant. Worse, the doctors gave no hope for improvement. "So terrible," Ah Ming murmured to herself, "the doctors don't know any more than me, a stupid country girl!"

Shao Lan could not hold her own chopsticks to eat and either could not or would not take care of her own body. But it was her perpetual attempts at suicide that required the most constant vigilance. The prospect of death seemed to be the only thing that could rouse her from her black torpor. At any unguarded moment, Shao Lan was likely to try to throw herself from a window or run from their courtyard into the busy street. Since Li Tai-tai was a schoolteacher, she could not stay with her daughter. So, to guard Shao Lan's life, she hired Ah Ming.

"Shao Lan." Ah Ming gently whispered the name and tried to press a pared wedge of apple into Shao Lan's limp hand. "Please eat. These are the sweetest apples of the season. Your mother will be so happy if you just eat a little."

Shao Lan allowed Ah Ming to lodge the fruit between her fingers but made no move to eat it. Eventually, it slipped to the cement floor and lay at her feet, a sticky prize for hunting ants.

"Ai-yah," Ah Ming sighed in exasperation. "Why do I trouble myself over you? You are hopeless." Ah Ming headed for the sagging wooden door, still clucking to herself. "I don't know why I worry about leaving you. You won't even notice I've gone."

With that, Ah Ming pulled the crossbeam across the door and headed carefully down the steep stairway. "Li Tai-tai," she called out. "I am leaving now. Your daughter is awake and locked upstairs. I will be back on the first of the month, as we agreed."

Although her departure was deliberately quick and casual, Ah Ming could not escape the sadness of leaving Shao Lan for the first time in a year.

Two days of telling each of her many cousins all about the wonders of Shanghai exhausted Ah Ming. But in all the excitement, she did not forget Shao Lan.

According to Ah Ming's mother, a certain sorceress in the village had the power to exorcise evil spirits. She made this power available to anyone with sufficient cash. "Oh, this is wonderful news," Ah Ming exclaimed. "I heard her family say this is the work of evil spirits! I will pay the sorceress. We should also take her many gifts. This is my mistress' only hope!"

"After all," her mother agreed, "this family has been so kind to you. This is the least we can do in return."

At the sorceress' gate, Ah Ming and her mother nervously eyed the paper demons that gaped and leered at them from faded posters flapping on the gateposts. A gaggle of villagers gathered around, in spite of the heat, curious to know what personal problems the gods would be petitioned to solve today. Whose family tragedy would be made public?

At last the rough, splintered portal with its chipped red paint and rusty, dragon-shaped latches swung open. A hunched old woman, swaying slightly on her tiny, bound feet, squinted at Ah Ming. With the flicker of an eyelid, she took in the content of Ah Ming's gifts and made a precise mental estimate of their market value. Satisfied, her mouth opened to let out a flash of gold teeth followed by a torrent of corrosive laughter.

"Come in, please come in. You must be the lucky girl just returned from the city. We must be a pitiable sight after the luxury you have, no doubt, grown accustomed to. Please forgive our miserable home. Come in, come in."

Ah Ming noticed the old woman actually twitching with eagerness to snatch the chicken she carried. She smiled graciously but held the chicken a little tighter. Her mother scowled, recognizing the innocuous welcome that threatened to set them up for the "city" rate. She countered.

"Thank you. Thank you for receiving a poor country woman and her worthless daughter so politely." They bowed and entered the courtyard.

As she watched the old woman totter before her, Ah Ming's hopes began to waver. Could this dusty relic of a witch contend with the stubborn powers that held Shao Lan?

"Are you sure you can help my mistress?" she blurted.

The old woman's eyes narrowed. "It all depends. The gods can be very demanding." She glanced at the rag knotted around Ah Ming's coins. "If you insult them, your mistress could get worse!"

Startled, Ah Ming tripped on the raised threshold.

The crone laughed. "I am not the one you came to see. It is my daughter who holds the magic now."

Ah Ming met the younger sorceress, a woman in her mid-forties, with great relief. From what she knew of these things, an exorcism required physical stamina as well as mystical clout.

The three of them sat on bamboo stools in a dim, inner room. Calligraphy banners, trimmed in red and gold, liberally papered the walls. Ah Ming wondered if the mysterious brush-strokes contained some special power. Or, as she couldn't help noticing, was this ornate display simply hiding the many cracks in the crumbling plaster walls? Tacked up on either side of the doorway hung two man-sized paintings of guardian spirits. Although the paper had long since curled and discolored, the fierce, grotesque expressions of the guardians were still effective. Ah Ming shuddered. At their feet, two incense pots paid homage. Coils of scent-laden smoke snaked upwards, then dispersed, until the entire room floated in a heavy, sweet grayness.

The sorceress sat up straight with her eyes closed. Slowly, she beat a small, wooden fish which sat on a pedestal at her knees. The steady rhythm gradually pulled them all into its hypnotic grasp. She began to sway and, without realizing it, both Ah Ming and her mother swayed with her. Gradually the sorceress merged her voice with the sound of the drum. Chanting incantations, she began to rock more violently. Finally she could no longer control her rhythm and abandoned the fish-drum. Tossing her head, her chant became interspersed with moans and she stood up. Suddenly, she started running in circles around the room.

"I have reached Hangzhou." She continued to run. "I am now in Shanghai. I am on a street with a long wall of iron posts. Now I am in a large garden with many trees. There is a trellis of jasmine behind the water pump . . ." And on and on.

Ah Ming's heart beat hard. The sorceress was describing her

mistress' street and courtyard exactly!

"Within this garden is a yellow building with two stories. I am going up a steep stairway. I am knocking on the door. It is opened by a short, middle-aged woman . . ."

That was Shao Lan's mother! Ah Ming trembled with both excitement and fear. Suddenly, the sorceress fell to the floor.

Appearing from the shadows, the sorceress' mother flew, wild with panic, to her daughter's inert body. Ah Ming cowered in the corner, terrified, as the old woman shrieked with fury.

"Why have you come here and harmed my daughter? You have enraged the gods! She has never fainted like this before. What have you done?"

Frantic, the old woman held her daughter's head and scratched with her fingernails, just below the nostrils. Wailing, she begged the gods to return her daughter's spirit.

Before her stunned and speechless customers could find words, the sorceress stirred. She was clearly exhausted but, seeing them still there, she began to scream.

"Get out! Get out of my house! Don't ever ask me to cast out a demon from that family again."

Ah Ming stared at her, bewildered.

"Your mistress comes from a family that has believed in Jesus for generations. I could not enter that house."

Ah Ming's heart sank in despair. "Is there any way for my mistress to be cured?"

The sorceress looked at Ah Ming for a long moment. Finally, she mumbled, "Only if they truly believe in Jesus . . . she will be cured."

With renewed rage, the older sorceress drove Ah Ming and her mother away with a flood of maniacal threats and scolding.

That night, Ah Ming stayed up to write a letter to Shao Lan's mother, Teacher Li. The kerosene lantern sputtered and mosquitoes whined close, like hungry fugitives lured from the darkness by the sight of food. Ah Ming's lack of education frustrated her as she struggled to put her simple words on paper. Her writing was clumsy and filled with mistakes. But this was so important! She bit down hard on her lip, forcing herself to concentrate and try again.

It was nearing the first of the month and Teacher Li held a letter from the servant girl in her hand. The many errors exasperated her. It was barely decipherable. Yet she sensed an urgency, a pleading that kept her from throwing it away. So here she was, late at night and alone, still trying to make sense of this crude missive.

She looked at the letter for what seemed like the hundredth time. Suddenly a complete, coherent sentence jumped out at her. Had she seen that before? It was clear and unmistakable!

"Only if you truly believe in Jesus, then your daughter will be cured."

The words stunned her and she began to cry. "I haven't prayed in years! I've forgotten all about God."

Teacher Li came from a Christian home but it had not taken long for an atheistic education and marriage to a non-believer to erode her faith. It was easy to ignore God when life was good. By the time Shao Lan's tragic illness struck, God was a non-occurring thought.

Now God himself confronted her. Not with condemnation, but with hope.

"God," she confessed, "I have forgotten you all these years and allowed Satan to come and take my child. But you haven't forgotten me. You have used this to bring me back to you."

Her heart broke and she wept freely.

The next morning, Teacher Li sought out some Christian relatives she vaguely remembered from childhood. She told her story and asked them to pray for Shao Lan's healing. On the following day, she brought Shao Lan with her.

At the threshold of the small Christian home, Shao Lan balked. Refusing to enter, she grew violent and convulsive. Finally her mother and others had to forcibly drag her into the house. In unison, they began to pray.

As they prayed, Shao Lan's struggles and screams subsided. Peace settled on her brow. Before long, gentle tears spilled down her cheeks, like the tears of a child finding comfort in her mother's arms at last.

EPILOGUE

In subsequent weeks, Christians throughout the area prayed earnestly for Shao Lan. Each time, she grew noticeably stronger and emotionally healthier. Her thoughts of suicide disappeared. Her interest in life returned. She wanted to eat!

Over the next two months Shao Lan made up over two years of missed schooling. Not only did she complete the work, but she passed her exams with scores high enough to win a place in the most competitive and prestigious school possible!

Today, Shao Lan and her mother meet regularly in a small house with other believers. They testify to many of the hope that is found in God, our Healer.

7 *Chapter* 柒

THE GIFT OF REVELATION

"As the rain and the snow come down from heaven, and do not return to it without watering the earth and making it bud and flourish, so that it yields seed for the sower and bread for the eater, so is my word that goes out from my mouth: It will not return to me empty, but will accomplish what I desire and achieve the purpose for which I sent it."
Isaiah 55:10–11

WE CAN LEARN all about meteorology and know all there is to know about rain and snow . . . but we cannot make it rain or snow. We are equally helpless when it comes to knowing God. Man is just as dependent upon God to reveal himself as he is dependent upon God to water the earth. Both are acts of grace.

That God would deign to reveal himself at all is a mystery of love. That he would reveal himself threefold—through his creation, through his Word, and through Jesus the Word Incarnate—is even more amazing. Yet in the arrogance of our intellect, we often set aside God's self-revelation and attempt to define him by our own imagination and fancy.

Our self-conjured gods are impotent apparitions with no power to bring forth life. When we simply let God speak for himself, and humbly accept his own revelation, our understanding becomes fruitful. His Word will birth new life.

THE HIDDEN GOSPEL

· 1973 ·

TWO MEN crouched perfectly still in the dark shadows of the pines, waiting for the moon to slip discreetly behind her veil of clouds. Just ahead, the shed door cracked open ever so slightly. The silent figures smiled, knowing their friend waited inside. They glanced around for anyone who might notice this strange rendezvous. As thick clouds blew in, they watched the patchwork of light and dark around them melt into a solid blanket of night. "Run for the shed!"

Crouching in the far corner of the shed, they lit a small torch. Their hearts pounded. Slowly, first one, then another, lifted a mud brick from the base of the wall. The third man returned to the door to stand guard. Finally, in the room's breathless hush, the first man cupped his hands around their treasure and pulled it from its secret hole in the wall.

It looked like nothing more than an old box. Ying Li held the rough, splintered wood while his friend, Ching Lu, reached in. It was still there! The three men huddled close and began to read from this strange and illegal book—the Book of Matthew.

· 1986 ·

Chiang Po urged his mule up the narrow trail, straight through the overhanging branches, then stopped to hold their sharp, snagging fingers aside for his honored guest. The elderly man rounded the steep bend below, his face covered with dust and flecks of bark. Sweat trickled down his temples and neck. He noticed Chiang Po waiting to clear his path and smiled.

"Please, it's not necessary to be so polite. I'm old but I'm not feeble."

Chiang Po laughed. "There are people in my village who have waited thirteen years for someone like you to come. If you arrive with even a scratch, I will be pig feed."

The old pastor, Wu Li Wen, pulled a small towel from his belt and mopped his face. Chiang Po, a fit mountain man, waited patiently. In the moment's pause, Pastor Wu marveled at their journey. Here he was, a 72-year-old man, riding into a remote region famous for generations only for its bandits and thieves. His young, exuberant guide certainly did not match any description ever made of the local inhabitants.

They had left the last bus and the paved road at four o'clock that morning. The red, iron-rich soil of the province coated the two men's clothing until they looked as if they had rusted in the rain. The late morning sun was hot and both men were tired. But an intense curiosity spurred Pastor Wu on and Chiang Po was anxious to deliver his guest.

Finally they stopped under an outcropping of large rocks, too hungry to continue. The gray slate pillars gave welcome shade away from the deep forest's profusion of flying, crawling hosts. Chiang Po produced a canvas satchel filled with pears and a pouch of "travelers' cereal," a combination of ground grains that he mixed with water into a rib-sticking porridge. The men ate silently and quickly, each thinking about the hours of daylight left.

At dusk they reached the high, western pass that cradled Ipu, Chiang Po's village. Plodding up the final switchbacks, they began to notice something strange. The wind carried more than the murmur of pine and cedar. They paused to listen. Far below, water rushed and tumbled through a granite gorge. A crow cawed in the trees. But there was something else.

They cleared the last rise and suddenly realized . . . voices! Hundreds and hundreds of them! Sloping away beneath them, the mountainside rippled in a sea of blue and white—the tribal dress of the Yi people. Like a late blooming of wildflowers, they covered every open space. Even Chiang Po was speechless.

Some had traveled for days. Some had left their home villages long before daylight. And since no one wanted to miss a word, they came early. Later, Pastor Wu learned they had been assembled, waiting and watching the trail, for over six hours.

With tears in his eyes, Pastor Wu scanned the crowd. His mind flashed back to his twenty-three years spent in a Communist prison camp. During his lowest moments, God had often spoken to him, telling him to hold on, for the time would come when he would be needed to teach the Word again. That promise had seemed so impossible! But here before him stretched fifteen hundred believers who had never had a teacher—waiting for him!

The hours rolled by into the night and still the old pastor taught. They lit torches and gas lanterns. No one wanted to go. At last, Pastor Wu's voice gave out and they allowed him to stop and sleep.

It was barely dawn when the sleeping multitude began to stir. Appearing like ghosts in the morning mist, they gathered around the heat of red-hot coals that glowed passionately in the arms of black, iron cooking braziers. Pots of boiling rice, donated by the Ipu villagers, gurgled and sputtered jets of steam into the cold mountain air.

Pastor Wu awoke in Chiang Po's home, a simple, mud-brick house with two rooms and a courtyard which served as a threshing floor. This morning, the courtyard quickly filled with neighbors and friends. Everyone had much to tell and many questions to ask.

No one had more questions than Pastor Wu. Weren't these the notoriously lawless and barbaric Yi people? For years, harsh government policies had failed to control or elicit cooperation from them. Why did he find them so different now from their reputation, worshiping God and longing to know more?

As Pastor Wu asked his incredulous questions, he could hear their embarrassed laughter.

"Let Old Lee tell you," a voice in the crowd offered. "He can tell you about the Book."

Others chimed in in agreement as an old, blind man emerged from the bustle. His friends cleared a path and gently sat him on a low stool before Pastor Wu.

"Old Lee," they urged, "tell the teacher about our Book."

Old Lee's face shone and burst into a radiant, toothless grin. In his arms he clutched a warped, splintering, shabby box. He held it as if it contained all the world's treasure.

"Teacher Wu," he began in a faint, rasping voice and immediately everyone fell silent. "Thirteen years ago, no one in this village knew about God. My brothers and I spent most of our time in drinking and gambling. We did not understand anything else. One day, I went down the mountain with my brother. I went to beg and he to steal. In the marketplace someone handed me this book."

Carefully, Old Lee extracted his prize possession. A small sheaf of coarse, brittle pages, long since yellowed and cracked, trembled in his hands. The pages were crudely stitched together, bound between two squares of dirty cardboard. Old Lee gently placed the book in the teacher's hands. Smiling and nodding, the villagers murmured their approval.

Pastor Wu had never seen a book so wretched and worn. He held it gingerly for it seemed it could crumble away with a breath. All around him villagers watched with tears on their rugged, brown cheeks. He had never seen a book so beloved!

"It is a part of something called Matthew," Old Lee offered. "Of course, we didn't know what it was when we got it. But after my brother began to read it, we decided it must be some kind of special book. So we hid it."

"Ah, yes," Pastor Wu sighed in understanding. Thirteen years ago, in the campaign against "intellectualism," no book was safe. Anyone who knew how to read was in danger of being branded as an "anti-revolutionary elitist"—a charge punishable by death.

"Did you know how particularly dangerous it was to have this book?" Pastor Wu asked.

Old Lee nodded gravely. "We knew. We knew it had foreign poison. We had to be very careful, especially after they sent the Party cadres to live in our village. At first, my brother and I were afraid. But then we showed it to a friend. He became so excited! He said we must keep it at all costs."

Pastor Wu wondered at such risk taken for a mere scrap of a book. "What did your friend know about it?" he asked.

Old Lee chuckled. "He was forced to attend a propaganda meeting staged for several villages. A man made a speech about the religion of this book. This man was once a convert but in his speech he said, 'The Christians claim that a man called Jesus Christ came to save mankind. This religion from overseas was brought here to deceive us.' Later, my friend learned that the Party had paid this man 2,000 yuan to forsake his belief and say this. But because of this speech, my friend was very curious to know more about Jesus Christ. When he saw our book, he said that somehow he knew it was a book of truth. He was the first one to believe. Then my brother, and then myself."

Old Lee paused in his narration while Chiang Po's wife placed a small, porcelain cup of scalding tea in his hand and graciously extended another cup with both hands to Pastor Wu.

Old Lee resumed. "At first, it was just the three of us. We hid the book in an empty shed, buried in the wall. Later, we brought a few others to read it, one at a time. Soon, ten of us were believers and we met in the forest at night to encourage one another and pray. We became 30, then 50 and 60." Old Lee cocked his head as if to tune in the sound of bodies pressing around him. "As you can see," he laughed and spread his hands outward, "our numbers have grown."

Chiang Po, barely able to contain himself to this point, now burst with excitement. "There are 1,500 of us now! Before, we worshiped demons. Now only one family in our valley is not Christian but they no longer worship demons either. We have heard about baptism. Do you know how to baptize?"

Carried on a wave of cheers, the news spread quickly. Clusters of people scurried to make preparations while others ran to tell those still on the hillside. "We're going to be baptized!"

That afternoon, in a high mountain stream under the blazing South China sun, Pastor Wu baptized almost 1,000 Yi tribespeople. The next day, he baptized hundreds more in a neighboring village. After two days more of continuous teaching, it was time to go home.

A torchlight procession escorted him for many miles in the pre-dawn darkness. At the paved road, Chiang Po and Wu Li

Wen embraced. Old Lee handed Pastor Wu a gift—the Book of Matthew!

"You may take this," he began. "Show it to others. At first we didn't want to give it up, but it is right that we share what God has done. Many people would scorn such a poor book, but they are seeing only the book. We see God's mercy in bringing it to us. Tell them this . . . that we have seen the mercy of God."

EPIILOGUE

Because the large Yi tribe is so widespread, Bible translators had been working on the Yi Bible for many years in other areas, particularly Thailand. In early 1989, Christians hiked up to Chiang Po's village with the first complete Bibles printed in the Yi language loaded on their backs. Today, many thousands of Christians meet throughout this remote region in dozens of small churches, all built by the local body.

Yi Christians have taken in all the elderly with no families. They have voluntarily funded and built several roads and bridges— projects that had frustrated the government for years because the Yi people were so wild and uncooperative. The witness of these acts has astonished the Communist officials and they are actually donating land for churches and arranging for electric power so the churches can have lights!

8 _Chapter_ 捌

THE GIFT OF HEALING

*"Praise the LORD, O my soul, and forget not all his benefits—who for-
gives all your sins and heals all your diseases, who redeems your life from
the pit and crowns you with love and compassion."* Psalm 103:2–4

THE AISLES of the mega-toystore are crammed with the
magical stuff of little girls' dreams. Mermaid dolls with long
flowing hair sit coyly on the shelf. Winnie-the-Pooh and his win-
some friends gather to share a miniature birthday party. I'm here
to shop for my own daughter's fifth birthday. I tell myself to keep
it simple.

But these merchandisers are good at what they do! I pick out
a Sesame Street tablecloth but soon find myself reaching for every
coordinating add-on—the hats, the balloons, etc., etc. I'm throwing more toys into the cart than I ever planned to buy. My mother's
heart keeps saying, "She'll love it!"

On the way to checkout, I look with shock at the brimming
cart. What came over me? Resolutely, I put back the excess. But
as I do, a smile comes to my heart. Jesus said, *"If you, then, though
you are evil, know how to give good gifts to your children, how much
more will your Father in heaven give good gifts to those who ask him!"* If
I have such a strong desire to bless my little girl, just imagine our
Father's heart towards us!

He is eager to give us the Holy Spirit, to restore, to redeem
and to heal. With great longing, he seeks to work mighty things
on our behalf. And our Father never has to put anything back on
the shelf, because the whole store is his!

FOREIGN GOD

MING JU knocked her head three times to the earthen floor. Her arms stretched upward with her palms pressed together to hold five sticks of smoldering incense. The impassive face of Buddha stared past her into the dark evening shadows. Ming Ju got up from her knees and approached the altar, keeping her head bowed and her eyes on the floor. Her hands stayed above her head until she reached a cracked, red lacquer bowl filled with sand. Then, with great care, she inserted each burning stick, forming a circle in the sand. Desperate prayers for her mother rose up in pungent rings of smoke. Ming Ju's mother was blind.

Ming Ju backed up, her head still bowed. She turned to the left corner of her little mud-and-thatch shrine. Again, she prostrated herself on the floor. From a high ledge, the village god glowered down upon her. The last glimmers of light caught the chipped white paint of his bulging eyes. It wasn't her fault. It was the Communists who gave no ration for temple paint. She fumbled in the pockets of her Mao jacket. Nestled in the torn padding, she carried two fresh eggs. She lifted them up, presenting them to the teakwood idol. Was it enough?

"Please, please," she whispered, "please accept my offering."

A cold fear began to creep through her body. She felt her chest tighten, as if bands of steel were being twisted around her by unseen hands.

"No," she wailed, "not this time. Please!"

It wasn't as if she was new to this. After all, she was the village witch. Countless times the spirits had come at her beckoning. They gave her power, and power excited her. It brought her status; the entire clan feared and respected her. But it was a power she could no longer control.

The pressure around her lungs grew unbearable and Ming Ju gasped for air. The eggs dropped and splattered on the ground. Suddenly she was thrown hard on her face and she felt blood trickling from her nose. She tried to scream but had no breath. Scrambling for the altar, she grabbed the small, sharp knife she had learned to keep for times like this. Clutching it with both hands, she drew it across her chest until blood ran down her smooth skin and soaked into her jacket. The pressure released. She could breath again.

Ming Ju returned to the house still trembling. She had to find bandages. She had to change before anyone saw her. Next time, she determined, she would bring the pig and slaughter it in the shrine. The pig's heart would bring strong magic. How could the gods not be pleased?

In the city of Kunming, in a small one-room apartment, an old woman knelt in a prayer of thanksgiving. A wide-brimmed, straw hat lay where it had been tossed in the corner, cocked on the corner of a stack of large-print Bibles. Bau Chen was so tired, but exhilarated at the same time! What a priceless treasure had come today! She checked the secret storeroom often, probably more often than was safe, and usually it was empty. But today . . . today the angels must have come! Actually, Bau Chen had no idea who made the sporadic deliveries. She only knew to keep checking, and keep praying. So many were waiting for Bibles, but she had a special place in her heart for the old women, those who had long ago lost their copies of Scripture during years of imprisonment. Who would have imagined that God would send large-print Bibles just for them? In her joy, Bau Chen laughed aloud. She grabbed her knee-high rubber boots out from under the bed and slapped on her hat. She had to keep the Bibles moving.

Bao Chen squeezed through the narrow passage that separated two tall buildings, trying to stay out of the gutter that ran between her feet. Her cotton backpack bulged to the tearing point. She had casually lashed a lumpy quilt over the whole bundle. Anyone passing by saw a grandmother carrying a sleeping child. She emerged at the corner of a busy intersection and immediately disappeared into a swarm of bicycles. The shrill clang of bicycle bells and shouts of street vendors drowned out her song. Bao Chen headed for the bus stop. She would deliver the Bibles in the city, navigating a maze of bus routes, lost in the crowd. Then she would head for the countryside.

The city wore a perpetual blanket of black soot, the effect of millions cooking on coal braziers. On the bus, passengers wore bandannas, gauze, torn strips of clothing, anything they could find, tied over their mouths to keep from choking as they jounced their way through crowded, potholed streets. Bao Chen pulled her scarf over her nose, grateful for the extra obscurity.

She glanced out the dirty bus window just in time to see three uniformed public-security officers turn the corner, heading toward the east quarter where she lived. Everything about them had grown familiar over the last two years—the way they walked, the way they fidgeted with their holsters, the arrogant cock of their heads when speaking to lesser beings. They searched her apartment regularly and called her in for questioning about every two months. In general, Bao Chen sighed, they were a nuisance. She perched on the edge of her bus seat, gripping the handstrap that hung down from the ceiling. She had to appear careful not to crush her "baby." Turning her head away from the window, her mischievous eyes crinkled in a smile. Once again, the police were too late!

At last, Bao Chen reached the city's outskirts. Her backpack no longer contained Bibles. It still bulged, but with a new set of gifts. Grateful hands had restocked it with oranges, beancakes, even chestnuts. She stepped from the last bus with new-found energy. It was a three-hour walk to the village but her stride was firm, strengthened by 20 long years in forced labor camps. She eyed the darkening sky and quickly assessed the puddled road. "Thank you, Jesus, for my boots," she murmured. This was where God had called her—to distant villages where superstition and demon worship were experiencing their own revival. And there was a particular woman she wanted to see today. A blind woman.

Ming Ju leaped from the door of her hut with a shriek. Something terrible was happening! She could feel it. She scratched at the scab that had formed across her chest, ripping at it until warm, sticky blood covered her fingers. "Get off me!" she screamed into the night at her unseen visitors. What did they want from her, anyway?

A lantern flickered from the cracks of her eldest brother's home. Faintly, she could hear her mother's voice. Other voices from the family occasionally interrupted. One woman's voice was new to her. The rest of the village had gone to sleep with the last light of dusk. Who was talking to her mother? Something inside her welled into an unexplainable rage and she felt herself driven across the courtyard.

As the door crashed open, the visitor, Bao Chen, turned. The woman standing against the black night glared at her with visible fury. But there was something else beneath the anger.

An old, blind woman, sitting before Bao Chen in the one-room hut, turned her head toward the sound of panting breath. "This is my daughter, Ming Ju."

"Don't be afraid," Bao Chen whispered gently.

"Afraid?" Ming Ju's voice shook. "Why should I be afraid of you? How dare you come bother my mother at this time of night? Get out!"

The blind woman lowered her head. "I'm sorry. Please forgive my daughter for . . ."

"Don't apologize for me, Mother." Ming Ju turned to her brother and sister-in-law as they tried to back away from their guest. "What's the matter with you, allowing strangers into your home at night? Who is she?" Ming Ju wasn't sure herself why she was acting this way. Why did she feel so . . . so invaded? So frightened?

Ming Ju's mother stretched out her tiny, wrinkled hand and motioned for her daughter to come closer.

"This is Mrs. Wong . . . Wong Bau Chen. She has come a very long way to see me. Her mother was a friend of mine a long time ago. Please listen to her." Her soft, thin voice faded to silence, like a kettle hissing its last breath of steam.

Her mother's gentle pleading softened Ming Ju's heart. But she was still suspicious and remained standing. She would listen . . . maybe.

Bau Chen turned to each member of the family in turn. "There is only one true God and he loves each one of you. Because he loves you, he has asked me to come and tell you about him."

They fidgeted, they mumbled, they shot veiled glances at one another. Indignation. How dare she tell them their gods were false? Curiosity. A god who loved them? There was no such thing. Gods were capricious and demanding, with a vicious streak that must constantly be appeased.

Bau Chen continued. "The true God has already proven that he loves you."

Ming Ju stamped her foot. "You are a babbling fool!" But secretly, something within her ached to hear more. Her heart was twisting on itself and she could not bear the torment. "Go ahead, tell your stories to the silly old woman if you want. I've heard enough." She turned and fled from the house. Alone, she whispered to the sky, "Is it true?"

Ming Ju did not sleep that night. She strained to hear the newcomer's voice, at once both repelled and drawn. She caught the word "missionaries" and instantly felt a renewed rage. So that's where this nonsense came from! What use did the Chinese have for another, foreign god? They had plenty of their own. She wondered at her own feelings, the anger of one whose hopes have been raised only to be crushed. *I must be a better Chinese*, she resolved. *I have not been devout enough.* She thought about the pig.

Before light, Ming Ju was up. In the quiet, misty dawn, her shadowy figure circled around the shrine, sprinkling a ring of bone ash. This would be the perfect sacrifice, she thought.

Bau Chen prepared to leave. The longer she was away, the harder it was to account for her time to those bothersome authorities. Clasping the blind woman's hands in her own, she smiled. "Now I know why my mother spoke so tenderly of you. I am so glad I came and I thank you for having me."

The old woman said nothing but Bau Chen could see small tears in the corners of her white-covered eyes.

"Don't worry," Bau Chen continued, "Jesus will stay with you. I'm the only one leaving!" She laughed, wanting to lighten the moment. She sensed the fear that lurked in this woman's darkness. "I know your daughter is angry. But you do not need to be afraid of her, or her gods. You belong to Jesus now and you can call on him anytime."

"Do you really think he will heal my eyes?" Her small voice trembled.

Bau Chen paused. They had prayed for these blind eyes last night, but still they did not see. She bowed her head down close to the old woman's face. "Grandmother, I promise I will keep praying for you."

On the long, hot walk back to the bus, Bau Chen thought of nothing but her visit. This blindness . . . what was God trying to tell her? She squinted into the blazing sky. Black crows skimmed the smooth, blue surface, then disappeared into a fiery cauldron of white light. "Ai-yah! she muttered. "What's an old woman like me doing walking in this heat?" She pulled the brim of her straw hat lower against the intruding glare. Yesterday's mud was already baked into thousands of separate puzzle pieces, the road crazed by jagged, miniature ravines. The surface crunched under her mud-caked boots. Alone with the scream of the birds and her own footsteps, Bau Chen quieted her heart and listened for God until she knew what to do.

The rise and fall of Ming Ju's chanting voice rolled through the village in hypnotic waves. Her drumbeat lifted and carried her voice from crest to crest. For most, it was a reassuring sound. The spiritist was doing her job, ensuring the well-being of their homes and families. Mothers clucked at young children, fathers boxed the ears of older ones, rousting them to the fields. The cadence continued, giving rhythm and reason to another morning already thousands of years old.

When the pig stopped squealing, the village stopped. Clansmen froze in knee-deep rice paddies and cocked their heads to listen. Young girls dropped limp hands into their washbuckets and looked, wide-eyed, for their mothers. The witch had killed her pig! The last animal with any meat on its bones had been eaten long ago—except this special one.

Crouched by the low entrance to the shrine, Ming Ju grasped the dead pig under his snout. Pulling his head backwards with one hand, she thrust a large ceramic bowl under his neck with the other. Hot blood poured into the bowl. As it filled and grew heavy, she dropped the pig and clutched the bowl with both hands. Her whole body trembled, making it hard not to spill her costly offering as she carried it into the shrine. She set the dark, swirling pool down on the altar already adorned with smoldering censers and fresh camellia blossoms. Never breaking her chant, Ming Ju stretched herself out flat and face-down in the dust. Her plaintive monotones grew more intense, swelling into mournful wails. She could feel them. Like the incoming tide, forces tugged and pulled at her soul, carrying her out into dark depths of the unseen realm. Her fingers clawed at the rocky floor until the raw tips bled. Hours passed with no awareness of time.

Late in the morning, a high scream tore through the hot, still air. Ming Ju appeared, reeling toward the cluster of village homes. Children cried and ran inside, innately sensing trouble. Ming Ju's face was blank and lifeless. Her eyes stared ahead, looking at nothing. She stumbled, then fell in the road. The sick-sweet smell of slaughtered pig immediately brought flies to her crumpled form.

No one touched her. No one even went into the road. No one wanted to come too close to what they feared. Only the blind woman came, her mother. The villagers watched from their doorways as the Old One tapped and groped her way to her daughter's body. They took uncomfortable peeks at the frail figure stooping to caress the witch's face.

Ming Ju groaned. "Mama . . ."

Thin, gentle hands cradled her bruised head. "Shh."

"Mama . . . it was everything I had . . . they laughed . . ." Her aching body rose and fell with silent sobs.

She hated the gods! No, that wasn't it, she realized. They hated her!

"Mama, I'm sorry . . ." Ming Ju drifted into the deep sleep of one who's life has been sucked from her bones.

Three days passed. Bau Chen had returned to the city. She

didn't know what God was going to do, but she knew he had told her to fast and pray. Two trusted friends joined her in the battle and they prayed for deliverance from darkness.

"Ming Ju! Ming Ju!" The thin, high voice penetrated Ming Ju's heavy sleep. Was it morning already? If she hadn't agreed to sleep beside her mother and care for her, she would have no reason to get up. What could she want so early? Ming Ju grumbled and reached across the woven, straw matting that served as their bed. "Mama, shh . . ."

"Ming Ju, my shoes!"

Ming Ju struggled to wake herself. "What about your shoes?"

"I can see them! There they are!"

Ming Ju bolted out of her cocoon of quilts and stared at her mother. The thick, white film was gone from her eyes. She followed their gaze to the floor. Sure enough, a pair of tiny cloth shoes lay in her mother's line of sight.

The old woman's sleepy face burst into a radiant smile that transformed each crinkle and crease into a wreath of joy. Her wispy, white hair fell like a soft halo around eyes that sparkled with excitement. Hungrily, she took in her daughter's beloved face, stroking her soft, brown skin and lightly caressing her straight, black hair. She giggled like a child.

"Ming Ju, you are still beautiful."

Ming Ju's eyes filled with tears. "Mama, you are still blind," she laughed.

Not until the shock of the moment passed did Ming Ju notice something else was different. Her mother's laughter was free and light. Like the early sun rising over the fields, it poured through the door and out the windows, flooding the house and driving away the shadows. In her heart, Ming Ju knew one thing to be certain. Her gods had not done this. She had invoked their power before and knew well that it came with a price. Their power never brought this kind of life; it took life away.

Her mother must have read her thoughts, for she took Ming Ju's hands into her own.

"I must say this, Ming Ju. Please listen. Jesus is real . . . he is the one who did this."

Her hands jerked from her mother's lap. She knew it was true. *Who was this foreign god? Why did he heal a Chinese woman?* She had so many questions! They had never burned one stick of incense in his honor or placed one offering before his image.

Suddenly, Ming Ju was afraid. *What would he demand for such benevolence?* They had nothing more to sacrifice.

Ming Ju chose her words carefully, not wanting to spoil her mother's happiness. "Mother, he must be a very powerful god . . . we have nothing left to pay . . ."

At this unexpected problem, a somber shadow passed over her mother's face. "I don't know . . . Bau Chen never said anything about that." Suddenly, her eyes rekindled. "She did say . . . she just said that he would be with me and help me."

This exasperated Ming Ju and she exploded. "Why? That makes no sense. You are a poor, unimportant old woman!"

She regretted her insulting words as soon as she said them, but facts were facts. Her mother was a fool to think it could be so easy.

Surprise and hurt registered on the leathery, lined face. Sheepishly, her mother twisted at the ends of her gown.

"Because he loves me," she barely whispered. "That's what Bao Chen told me. And now I believe her."

Ming Ju just stared, speechless, into her mother's sparkling eyes. It seemed as though years had lifted from her brow. Tight, pinching lines around her mouth relaxed into a shy, new smile. Ming Ju felt her throat tighten. She didn't want to cry. She didn't dare believe this, but suddenly she wasn't so sure she knew anything at all about gods . . . at least, not this one.

"Mother," her voice trembled, "let's go visit Bao Chen. I need to talk to her."

The tapping at the door didn't sound like the usual, insistent demand of the security police. Nevertheless, in one sweeping glance, Bau Chen quickly checked the room. Her boots were clean. Her backpack smelled of warm fruit and scallions.

Satisfied, she called out, "Wey?"

An uncertain silence followed. Bau Chen jumped up. It was probably someone come to ask for a Bible, someone standing in the alley, afraid they had come to the wrong door. Police never hesitated. She yanked at the bolts and poked her head out.

"Teacher . . ."

A tiny, bent figure lifted her face and Bau Chen found herself looking into two clear, smiling eyes.

"Grandmother!" Bau Chen's arms flew into the air. "Lord Jesus, thank you, thank you!" She couldn't take her eyes off the old woman's face, even as she bustled them in with a flurry of hugs and stream of chatter. What a glorious day! With great excitement, she dragged out her one chair and patted her bedding smooth.

"Please sit, please sit," she urged, giving her quilt a final, perfecting smack. "This is wonderful." Suddenly, she was aware of Ming Ju, still standing and obviously uncomfortable. "Ming Ju, I'm so grateful to you for bringing your mother to see me. I feel honored that you would share this happiness with me."

Ming Ju relaxed. This teacher of the foreign god did not hate her, even though she had been so horrible to her. Her fragile, seedling hope grew a little stronger. Maybe what her mother said about this god was true. Suddenly, everything that had been building in her heart wanted to burst out. She sank to the bed and could only cry, overwhelmed by her own emotions.

Bau Chen held her. As Ming Ju wept, Bau Chen spoke softly, telling her about a God who loved her.

"I don't understand," Ming Ju finally whispered. "I never made any sacrifice to this god. How could this be?"

Bau Chen looked into the young woman's haunted eyes, aged beyond her years. She could see telltale scars edging above the collar of Ming Ju's blouse. Bau Chen sensed the witch's total confusion. This woman had no reference point to help her understand a God of love. In her mind, Bau Chen searched for a way to put the love of Jesus in terms Ming Ju would understand.

"Ming Ju," she finally explained, "a very great sacrifice has already been made. The perfect sacrifice."